T0193224

TRUCK
OF
POTATOES

AN AUTOBIOGRAPHY OF
THERESA LANDRY

WRITTEN AND COMPILED BY
LYNDA NAGLE

Order this book online at www.trafford.com
or email orders@trafford.com

Most Trafford titles are also available at major online book retailers.

Print information available on the last page.

ISBN: 978-1-4907-7515-9 (sc)
ISBN: 978-1-4907-7517-3 (hc)
ISBN: 978-1-4907-7516-6 (e)

Library of Congress Control Number: 2016918201

Trafford rev. 11/08/2016

www.trafford.com
North America & international
toll-free: 1 888 232 4444 (USA & Canada)
fax: 812 355 4082

ABOUT THE AUTHOR

Theresa Landry is a woman of many words, all of them said with love and feeling. Ms. Landry immigrated to the United States from New Brunswick at 1 ½ years of age and never let life stop her from achieving her goals, no matter what obstacles she faced. She continues to set goals for herself at her current age of 94 (95 in November). No one has ever said one negative word about Theresa, mainly because she has never been one to say anything derogatory about anyone in her lifetime. And she certainly has had more than ten people's share of friends and acquaintances over the years.

In this autobiographical novel, Theresa shares some of her lifetime experiences, her many travels to unique places throughout the world, her meetings with famous people and the strange ways in which she met them, her feelings regarding the men in her life, her love of family and students and how she attained all that she did during the course of her life by being frugal and determined.

BOOK SUMMARY

This autobiography was recanted with words of love. The novel begins before Ms. Theresa Landry was even conceived with the meeting of her mother and father in New Brunswick. Their love grew into a marriage and a family followed by their immigration to the United States which became Theresa's journey through life.

Theresa's tales sprout from how she was raised and educated and how the lessons she learned through the guidance of this loving couple enabled her to blossom into a woman who made her way in life on her own and in her own way.

The vignettes recall the people in Theresa Landry's youth, her jobs, her recitals, her passion for dance and her students, her marriage, her daughter, grandchildren and great grandsons, her shows and the famous people she met along the way, along with interesting travels, literally and figuratively, each guaranteed to produce tears, laughter and love in any reader's heart.

CHAPTER 1

STRAWBERRY FESTIVAL TIME

During the month of August, the village of St. Andre in Canada would hold an annual strawberry festival. The young girls from the village would create specialty baskets containing farm cooked delicacies, such as pork sandwiches, fruit, pickles and mouthwatering bakery goods made by the girls' own hands. The handle of the basket was decorated with a large fluffy bow. Included was the drink of choice – good, old-fashioned lemonade. The boys gathered around the area, waiting anxiously for the bell to ring, signaling that they could go to the picnic tables and stake their claim for whatever basket they had chosen. Best of all, the young girl was part and parcel of that prize.

Simaire was a young lady, approximately 20 years of age, an excellent cook with a handsomely beautiful face and long, dark hair that flowed with ease around her shoulders. Patrick had seen Simaire at church services and when she would venture into the village, but he was always reticent to approach her. It was at least a half hour walk between their parents' farms, and it would be difficult for Patrick to see her too often.

But today was Patrick's opportunity. He had done his detective work well and knew which basket was Simaire's - #18. At the sound of the bell, the young man ran toward the basket with a smile on his face. Patrick's determination won him basket #18 and, eventually, Simaire's hand in marriage.

CHAPTER 2

AN ANGEL IS BORN

Simaire and Patrick were married at St. Joseph's Church one year after the festival. Simaire looked beautiful in her high-necked wedding dress. The long sleeves had cuffs adorned with a line of tiny pearl buttons. A small train swirled around the bottom of the dress lightly covering the floor tiles. The young lady was tall and had a thin waist which was accentuated by a large bow sewn on the back of the gown. Simaire made her own veil which consisted of two pieces of netting gathered atop her head forming the shape of a rose and flowing down the back of her torso. Handmade, simple, yet elegant. Patrick was formally dressed in a dark tuxedo, a white shirt and a perfectly shaped bow tie. He had a full head of black hair with a slight wave which made him look very dapper. Perfect for this ceremony of love.

During the first year of their loving, happy marriage, Simaire found herself pregnant. A baby boy was born. They called him their "little miracle." However, God had other plans. The tiny little boy caught pneumonia when he was but two months old. Without much heat and no medicine, he passed quickly. Both parents were grief-stricken. Patrick went to work making a small wooden coffin from oak trees, painfully weeping as he hammered each nail. Simaire lined the coffin with satin and made a pint sized pillow for the baby's head to rest upon, a soft spot upon which her son would be placed.

Following a Mass of the Angels, Simaire and Patrick placed the small coffin between them on the seat of their farm horse and buggy, slowly making their way up the hill where they would bury their infant son. Patrick had also made a small cross decorated with flowers which he hammered into the earth. Neither spoke, both shamelessly allowing their tears to tell their feelings. After a while, Simaire looked at Patrick and told him not to worry. There would be another son.

This picture resembles the buggy which carried the coffin to its final destination.

CHAPTER 3

THE PIONEER DAYS ARE OVER

For the next few years, Simaire and Patrick maintained their homestead on the family farm where Patrick developed a passion for working with his hands as a master carpenter. His main job was to bring a truck of loose potatoes to the village to sell in order to put food on the table for his family. By this time, Simaire had given birth to two daughters, Irene and Theresa. I AM THERESA!!!

My mother and father were ready to migrate to the United States. "Pop" had met a man in the village whom he referred to as his "pen pal." The man came from Sanford, Maine to buy produce from the farms across the border. After many conversations, he told my father that if he was not happy on the farm, there was plenty of work for him in Maine as a handyman, particularly in carpentry. Pop was elated. This was his chance to live in a big city and follow his dream.

My "Mom," Simaire, was the one with the knowledge of how they could accomplish this task together with two children and a baby on the way. According to Canadian law, only the parents and one child were allowed to pass through immigration and enter the United States of America. My mother might have been educated only until the eighth grade, but her common sense made her the woman she was. The plan she devised centered on the potato truck. My father filled it to capacity. My sister, Irene, was four and a half years old; she would sit on my mother's lap. I, at one and a half years old, was told by my Mom that I had to hide in the truck, deep under the potatoes with only a small opening around my little head from which I could breathe. If I dared to cry, we would all be sent back. My mother swaddled me in a comfortable wool blanket to keep me warm and content. After she would tell me this story when I got older, she would always end by saying, "It worked! You slept all the way to Maine."

CHAPTER 4

FROM MAINE TO RHODE ISLAND

Sanford, Maine became our new home. There were still only 4 of us because my mother had had a miscarriage due to making the trip. But by the time Irene was 6 and I was 3, baby Bertha made her way into our family. She was distinctive from the rest of us with her blonde locks. My Pop now had 3 daughters, not the son to replace Alfred. It was never meant to be. Mom had a total of 11 pregnancies and miscarried 8 times.

My father found work in Maine, but life was different. Men would walk by and see him tirelessly hammering away and they would stop and talk with "Pat." Once again, conversations ensued about a city in Rhode Island called Central Falls that was in the process of building huge churches and schools. They could use a worker like Pat, he was told. By this time, my father had a car. He and my mother packed us up and we were on our way to the smallest city in the smallest state in the Union.

Designing became my father's life. His most famous buildings were St. Edward's Church on Weeden Street in Pawtucket, and Hunt Street School on Hunt Street in Central Falls. I was so proud of my Pop. When the ribbon cutting ceremony was held for the opening of the church, he told me he wanted me by his side. I beamed with joy.

These accolades would have been enough for some men, but my father was a lifelong learner. He continued his education at night, taking home courses in design and drafting. He even studied the Palmer method to have perfect penmanship. I still have the papers that he wrote on to prove how meticulous he was with his work.

Mother, Irene, me, and Bertha who was sleeping inside the baby carriage.

Here I am posing with Bertha. It must have been a Sunday, dress day.

CHAPTER 5

HOW I GOT TO BE ME

I always did what I was told. After we had been living in Central Falls for about a year, the Depression began. It was 1928. My father needed money on which he could rely for the family to survive on a weekly basis. He was offered a job working for the W.P.A. where he earned $3 per week which covered the food, heat, electric and rent. We were living on Pine Street where I shared a room with my two sisters. We all slept in one bed with me in the middle. My sisters kept me warm.

One very cold wintry night, the snow was falling heavily. My father's job was to stand over an open hole in the road so that any car coming wouldn't hit the pothole. One flame for warmth and sight was in the middle of the hole. My mother came into the bedroom because she was so worried about Pop being outside all night. Out of the three of us, she knew she could count on me to understand her feelings. She told me to go to the Notre Dame Church Rectory, ring the bell and ask the priest for money to buy my father long underwear; otherwise, he would die from the cold. I dressed quickly and ran to the church. After I told him my plight, the pastor said, "Come in, child. I have three dollars that I can let you have for your father. But do not come back for any more. There is none." I ran to "Burns," a store on Dexter Street, and brought the long johns home for my Mom to fill with newspaper in the legs, back and body. "This," she said, "will keep your Pop warm." I felt better having helped.

I discovered there were other ways for me to help. Pop had been a step dancer in New Brunswick. Every evening, the men would gather in the kitchen, move the table and chairs to the sides of the room, and each would challenge the other to perform a different, more difficult step. Patrick was known to be the best! Watching him when I was little instilled my yearning to teach young children to dance. I would go with Pop to Saturday Night Socials at The Circle Canadian on Sylvian Street, The Eagles Club on Earl Street and The Elks Club in Pawtucket. I would be dressed with a little bow on the top of my head, a ruffle party dress and, of course, my tap shoes. On Sundays, the taps would be removed so I could walk down the aisle in church to receive communion without people hearing the clicking sound. My father would remove the nails and the taps for mass and school. He would replace the holes from the nails with cardboard, and the clicking sound would be gone.

At the clubs, the men would whistle and through pennies at my feet. I felt mortified. It was humiliating to be picking up pennies, but Pop said, "You have to. Five pennies will buy us bread; fifteen pennies will get us milk." I had an idea to, at least, make me LOOK like someone famous and restore my dignity. I went to Heroux's Funeral Home and managed to get Mr. Heroux to give me an old damaged top hat. I fixed it as well as I could, then asked Pop to make me a cane. Finally, I felt as if I looked professional. I would dance my heart out and did what I was told. I picked up the pennies.

It was the beginning of my career!

CHAPTER 6

STEPS IN MY EARLIER DAYS

Around the ripe old age of 10, I started my first small business. My father built a hardwood rollup platform to dance on which I would put in my little wagon. I went from house to house offering ½ hour dance lessons for 10 cents. I did this every day after school and developed a small clientele which would oftentimes get me back into the house after dusk.

A sense of true entrepreneurship began at age 13. We were now living on Perry Street. Neighbors could hear the click of tap shoes on the porch all summer, and in the winter, I taught on our hardwood parlor floor. My keen sense of business kicked in when I noticed that the bar across the street on the corner of Phillips and Perry Streets never opened until noon. I mustered up the courage to approach the owner, asking if I could use his bar as a studio from 9a.m. to 11:45a.m. I knew that it was important that no children be in the area when the bar opened. He agreed and charged me $2 per day. Obviously, I had to up my lesson fee to 25 cents considering I had rent to pay. My clientele steadily grew. The mirrors over the bar facing the door and the shiny hardwood floors were a definite upgrade.

During these early years, I knew it was important to the students to perform in the public eye. This gave them something to strive for, and I looked forward to our mini-"recitals." We performed in minstrels at both St. Mathieu and Notre Dame Churches. I would dance in the middle and the children would dance around me. The exposure was wonderful. My name was in the programs, and my "little ones" were a great sense of pride for me and for themselves.

These lessons continued through my high school years. My first and ONLY passion was teaching dance; but I was aware of the fact that I needed to work to make money to achieve this goal. I applied for a job listed in the newspaper for a bookkeeper/typist for a father/son painting company. I misunderstood the father as saying the hours were from 5 a.m. to 5 p.m. when he said 8 to 5! But I needed the money. For 12 hours a day I would work on the books, then be expected to clean the house, wash the curtains and do any other inside-the-house task that these two men found for me. The father's wife had died ten years previous which was the reason for such filth. I became totally disgusted and decided that standing in the unemployment line would be better than what I was putting myself through in a dirty house with an equally as dirty mouthed man.

This was the best move I made.

Here I am giving a 25 cent lesson to Roger Tougas. I was 14; he was 3. He became a priest. See the wooden floor my father made?

CHAPTER 7

BOND GIRL

After just a few days standing in line for unemployment benefits, I was told about a position for a typist at the Brown and Sharpe Company. I applied and met with a man named Mr. Earkhart who was very impressed that I was a high school graduate. He offered me the job that day. I neglected (purposely) to admit that my typing skills were far from stellar, but I knew that my personal speaking skills would more than compensate.

One day, after a few months of pathetic typing and desk hopping to talk with the other girls, I heard my name called over the intercom. "Would Theresa Landry please report to Mr. Earkhart's office?" I sadly wished all my new friends the best, saying my goodbyes, knowing this was it. I was being fired! I walked in to face the music, and I heard, "Miss Landry, I hear you are a rather good dancer. I have an accordionist and a singer. All I need now is a dancer to sell Government bonds on Fridays. Could you do that?" Was he kidding? Not only did I quickly blurt out "Yes," but I also pointed out that I did not have any money to buy stockings. I would need time to paint my legs tan and there would have to be another employee standing by to draw the stocking line up the backs of my legs to make the "stockings" look real. I told the boss I needed 2 hours to complete this process plus put on my costume (2 hours less typing for me!). I was a wheeler and a dealer even back then. This saved my job. After the singing and dancing, I walked around asking, "Hey, boys, any bonds today?" This continued every Friday.

My new friends at Brown and Sharpe turned out to be a fun-loving bunch. And my mother aided in their joie de vivre. The year was 1942. I was fortunate to have my own car, a 1936 Plymouth, in which I could fit quite a few people. Mom had a habit of deciding to do things on a whim. There were never many plans made, just her saying, "Let's do this next week." With the war going on, one of Mom's favorite non-planned activities was her telling me to get 4 girlfriends from work and 4 boys from the "Girls' City Club" in Providence. The club was a place for sailors who were on leave to go to and play cards, listen to the radio, eat and scout out the Providence area. My mother insisted that this party be formal. The girls would wear my gowns from the shows I had put on. As they dressed, they would be giddy from all the feelings of glamour and excitement. The boys looked very proper in their uniforms. Mother served alcohol-free punch (loaded with oranges, lemons and limes), homemade cupcakes and popcorn. We owned a Victrola (record player) which had to be cranked to play music which allowed us to dance the night away. The bewitching hour that ended the party was 11 p.m. at which time I drove the boys back to the club.

To me, being with these people was like getting a college education. The boys would tell stories about all the countries they had been to, and the girls and I talked about all the places we wanted to go to. I guess I could be considered the instigator for some of the trips we took. There was a sign on a building just down the street from Brown and Sharpe which read "Cash Here - $40." I told the girls how much fun we would have going to a ski lodge in New Hampshire. And we did! But the money wasn't so easy to pay back. We had each borrowed the $40 which covered the cost of the train, room and food. It might have been considered expensive and frivolous at the time, but my mantra continued throughout my life – "It was well worth the trip."

While working at Brown & Sharpe, I modeled the uniforms and made the belts on the machines.

Here I am posing in front of my 1936 Plymouth.

CHAPTER 8

THE FEET GO ON

Working behind a desk never stopped my mind nor my feet from moving and hearing the sounds of clicking tap shoes. When I was younger, my main source of enjoyment and learning came from saving my pennies to get a dime to go to the Lafayette Theater on Broad Street. I paid close attention to the dance steps the stars performed on the big screen. I would sit through movies twice to remember each one, as I choreographed the movements in my mind. My feet moved to the feet of Ann Miller, Judy Garland and Ginger Rogers, but Shirley Temple was my favorite. The length of her routines was proof of her marvelous memory at such an early age.

As I got older and could afford lessons, I found two very good dance teachers in Pawtucket, Doris Gagne and George Morin. Doris' style resembled that of a chorus line. She came from New York and charged quite heavily for a private lesson. If you paid a lesser amount, you could dance in the groups. This is what I could afford, and I still managed to watch intently and learn. Unfortunately, I was totally intrigued by Morin's intricate, individual steps, like the buck and wing. He had the suave Gene Kelly style. However, having attended Catholic schools and having a staunch Catholic mother, I was not allowed to take lessons from a man.

A few years later, when able to make my own decisions, I heard of a Black male dance teacher in Boston, Stanley Brown. I took the train from Central Falls to Boston to study under Stanley. He was an excellent teacher who gave me the best advice at the time.

"To be a good teacher and to make money," he said, "you need, at least, a 4 room studio." He taught in an old house that had 2 rooms upstairs and 2 rooms down. Stanley would circulate from room to room, show his students a new step to practice, then begin the routine again. His fee was $25 an hour. Mr. Brown was a good dancer and a great businessman.

I was learning, but teaching all this time, too. At the conclusion of 3 years at Brown and Sharpe, making $13 a week, I had enough students and enough money to be able to begin my dream of being a full time dance teacher. I followed Mr. Brown's advice and worked my way up to renting a studio that had 2 rooms. It was on the corner of Broad and Cross Streets where there is still a red light. When I left the front room curtains open, people could see in as they stopped their cars. Unbeknownst to the owner of the building, Mr. Whalen, this location was of monumental importance for my gaining so many new students. As it turned out, it was the perfect time to move on to bigger and better. Also, I had two girls as well as myself teaching. By this time, I had taken lessons from a variety of dance teachers to learn all the latest steps, and I had followed the advice of many wise people in the business. Stanley Brown was right.

These little girls are two of my very first students at the Broad Street studio.

CHAPTER 9

TIMES OF R & R IN NEWPORT

I am not a person now and never have I been someone who does not take advantage once in a while of a brief respite from a hectic life. These mini-breaks have always been a source of rejuvenation for me. I had a strong love for the beach, especially Second Beach in Newport. The beach and walking down the streets in Newport were a treat. My older sister, Irene, had met and married a man from Newport which led me to knowing my way around quite well.

I had noticed a quaint boarding house in the city. A woman named Mrs. Peckham was the owner. She charged 5 dollars a night, without breakfast. I spent many a night there enjoying the air. On a walk one day, I found another boarding house with a cute fence surrounding it. It was right near St. Mary's Church where Jackie and John Kennedy were married. I decided to rent a room there for a change of pace. The house had a porch where I would stand and enjoy watching the children play in the schoolyard at the convent across the street. The school was run by the Sisters of Cluny, and the nuns would always wave and say hello.

One day an Ensign in the Navy went running into the convent to say that his wife was about to give birth to their fourth son. He asked if they could recommend someone to stay at his home to take care of the other three until she came home from the hospital. After we had spoken, the nuns recommended me, knowing how much I loved children. This was another fun experience in my life, and it felt good to be doing someone such a favor. Getting paid for my efforts was a plus besides.

As it turned out, the owner of the boarding house had a best friend by the name of Mrs. Stevenson whose son was coming home on leave from the Air Force. The two women decided that Joe Stevenson and I would make a great couple, and they fixed it up for us to meet when he came home. The date went well, and Joe wrote to me regularly after his short visit was over.

I'm loving the summer months whether it be lounging in my bathing suit...

... or rowing on a lake.

CHAPTER 10

FIRST COMES LOVE, THEN...

1945 – The war had ended. Men were coming back to their families, those who had made it back, that is. I hadn't heard from Joe. When I did find out that he had returned, I still didn't hear from him for several days. I decided to take a ride to his parents' home in Newport. His father and I saw Joe lumbering down the street, almost toppling over. "Wonder how long THIS had been going on," his father uttered, sadly. I had no idea what he was talking about. A lot of men came back from the war "shell-shocked." That's what it was called back then. Now the letters PTSD (Post Traumatic Stress Disorder) are used referring to the variety of ways that trauma manifests itself.

Joe and I became exclusive, and I loved him for being such an intelligent, honest and gentle man. Yet...I should have known. Joe had attended U.R.I. to study pre-med. But the war interrupted his dreams. I became Mrs. Joseph Stevenson (a.k.a. Theresa Landry) on June 21st, 1947. Our marriage was not consummated immediately, and that worried me. Didn't Joe find me attractive? Did he love me, like he said? I was so upset that, finally, I decided to have a talk with his mother. I was more than surprised when this, what I thought to be, classy Newport woman looked me in the eye and laughingly said, "He'll find it eventually. Don't worry." These were not exactly the words I was expecting to help me understand the situation.

I guess my mother-in-law was right because the love of my life, Susan Brenda Stevenson, was born on March 2, 1949. I was still teaching on Broad Street until Susan's birth, and because I was so active, I only gained 12 pounds. Joe was a loving and doting father and became a house husband in order for me to return to teaching. Six weeks had passed, and I needed to start bringing money into the house again. Joe was not working.

Soon after, I moved the studio to the upstairs part of the LeRoy Theatre, a little farther down Broad Street. The owner allowed the students to perform on the large stage when movies were not being shown. It felt like my students were Hollywood stars, as they walked through the glitzy, shiny curtains that hung from the rafters. I never charged a dime for any of the shows. Anyone who came had to bring a canned good to donate to the poor. Each time, we performed before a full house. Again, it was great advertising which led to more students. Unfortunately, I was told I had to find a new place because the bookkeeper who also had a room in the theatre could not stand the sound of the tapping shoes.

My next and last move was to the Dexter Street studio where I remained for 63 years. Initially, I had one dance room and a small front desk/waiting space. Then the jewelry shop on the same floor closed, and I rented two more rooms. Finally, a man named Herve Fournier, a sign designer, died which allowed me to take the last two rooms. I had reached my goal of five rooms and an office. I had four teachers working for me, all having previously taken lessons from me, so I knew them and their styles very well. I also hired an excellent male acrobat from Fall River for the acrobatic lessons.

One day, a woman came in with her young daughter who wanted to take tap lessons. Her name was Ann. Years passed and she became a wonderful teacher and friend to my entire family. Ann stayed with me for about 20 years, eventually renting space in the studio for $17 a month. She left to open her own dance school. There were many girls who worked for me over the years who opened successful studios. And these women remain some of my best friends.

The teachers who should be commended for staying by my side for so long, taking lessons, teaching for me and for opening their own studios are: Gail Laxton, the most patient teacher who, no matter how sick she was, never missed a day of teaching; Gloria Dorais Brouilette, a wonderful teacher who took lessons from the age of 6 and began teaching for me at age 12, an accomplished tap dancer with a great personality; Donna Carter and Fran Golombiewski who both remain my good friends and call me often to go out to dinner or attend someone's show; Kim Audette who danced her heart out and came with me so many times to see the Rockettes in New York; and Sheila Parker and the Pickard twins, all adorable girls who worked very hard. I thanked them over and over for their dedication to teaching.

Joe and I looking so proper on our wedding day.
We didn't even drop a crumb of cake.

This picture is after a recital in 1949, 2 months before Susan was born.

INTRODUCTION TO VIGNETTES

The previous chapters of this book have introduced the people in my life before I even knew them, before I was born. But they and the situations that brought them together and made them my parents are what molded me into who I became. It should be obvious that there was a great deal of parental love, strong personalities and artistic talent in my background.

There are so many stories that I have to share that are a result of my upbringing, my home, schools I attended and my Catholic faith that the only way to do them justice is to continue the remainder of the book in vignettes. These stories are a compilation of moments, days, weeks and years of feelings. These feelings exude a range of happy, sad, bittersweet, tender, determined and loving – all parts of me that show a person who refused to give in to the negative side of life. My positive attitude has always prevailed.

I will attempt to categorize my stories into ones that refer to my family, my love of travel, my passion for dance and teaching dance, my naïve nature, my business sense and all the people I met as a result. ENJOY!!!

A SERIES OF VIGNETTES

EXAMPLES OF BEING NAÏVE...TAKE ONE

1. The snow in winter meant good sledding at Jenckes Park in the small city of Central Falls. It was one of my favorite fun pastimes with friends, but it also proved to be a time of personal fear. The boys would walk to the park with their sleds in tow. We would all meet at the top of the hill, and the boys would offer the girls the ride of their lives over the small hills to the end of the trails. There was a slight catch. The girls were to sit in the front of the sleds, so the boys could gallantly hold them to keep from sliding off. It was where and what they held on to that bothered me. After having a boy touch my breast, even though I had pajamas and a ski suit on, I was a nervous wreck! Worrying that I was pregnant, I would go home and count the months. No one talked to you about sex back then or how you had babies. It was not an open topic for discussion, except maybe with a real close friend. And, even then, she wasn't sure either!

2. The next scenario began with my mother announcing that we were going to a Polish picnic that took place annually at Governor Notte Park in North Providence. The man who ran the concession stand had a cute son named Steve who cooked and served the Polish food with his father. Steve had been watching me all day, smiling, flirting. He saw me dancing to the accordion player's music. Steve came over, we talked for a while, and he asked me to go to the movies. On the night of the date, he picked me up and drove directly to Lincoln Woods, known as "Lovers' Lane." I asked, "What

are we doing here?" "It's too early to go to the movie," he answered, and he began kissing my forehead and sucking on my ear lobes. When his hands landed on my breasts, I had to think fast. We were in a wooded spot. What could I do to stop him? I blurted out, "Oh, look at that cross in the sky! It's coming straight at us! Can't you see it?" I was so afraid; all I kept doing was repeating those words. Finally, Steve said, "What cross? I don't see a cross! Jesus Christ, you're going home. You're nuts!" He was nothing but a handsome showoff, and I was a lucky girl. After, when I would see him, he would shake his fist at me, probably because I was making the sign of the cross at him.

3. I always enjoyed every style of dance, particularly with boys as I got older. I went to places in Central Falls, such as, The Colonial Hall on Broad Street, The Polish Club on High Street and Palin's Ice Cream Parlor where we would put nickels in the juke box and dance until our coins ran out. At The Colonial Hall, if you got there early, a man named Professor Murphy would teach dances, like the waltz and the jitterbug, to those who didn't know them. The boys who went came from Sacred Heart Academy and the girls from my school, Notre Dame. One night I was dancing close with a boy who kept pulling me closer. I felt something pressing against my body. I had yet to learn how a man was built. The boy asked, "Why are you pulling away from me?" Not knowing what that hard thing was that I was feeling, I answered, "You've got to move your key chains."

4. In some respects, this lack of sexual knowledge lasted through to my days at Brown and Sharpe. The way our desks were placed had us in rows and face to face with each other with the fronts of the desks touching. I noticed a man who sat diagonally across from my desk staring at me quite often. One day, I felt a weird vibrating feeling and looked across only to see his desk practically jumping up and down. I stared at him this time wondering what was going on. A woman sitting next to me said, "Theresa, don't you know what he's doing?" Realizing that I didn't, she

informed me that he was "j---ing off." My face got beet red. I couldn't believe this was happening. The woman told me to tell the boss. I couldn't, but, obviously, someone did. He was fired the next day.

Being naïve in my young life was both a blessing and a curse. It was a source of worry at times, yet it also made me think fast. I believe this to be part of what has kept me sharp and on my toes all these years.

THE 40'S

The 1940's were a time of work for me, day and night. I had my job, the studio and U.S.O. shows. Agents for booking acts in nearby areas would place ads in the newspapers which is how I got in touch with Cliff Eddy. He found plenty of dancing jobs for me, but he was pushy from the start. After hearing my name, the first thing he told me was, "That has to be changed." To him, "Theresa" sounded too saintly, so I became "Terry Lane." Another common phrase Cliff used was "no baggage." That was in reference to my mother, a jolly soul who loved to go everywhere with me, mainly to get out and be sociable. She was not what one would call a "homebody," nor a "shrinking violet," for that matter. But, Cliff was in charge and I needed to make money. He got $6.00 per act and I got $3.00, plus a ride back to the Kennedy Plaza in Providence where we would meet.

The shows were in dining and dancing clubs and restaurants, all far enough away to need a ride. Some of the spots that may be recognizable were: The Valencia in Johnston, Valley View Car on Prospect Street in Valley Falls where I performed two shows a night for $6.00 at 8:00 and 10:00p.m., The Sportsman's Lodge in Pawtucket, The Golden Slipper in Valley Falls, The Cabbage Patch in Pawtucket, The German Haufbrau in Pawtucket, Bob's Tavern in Cumberland, the Cheerio Café in Pawtucket, The German Club in Pawtucket, The Ambassador Inn in North Providence, Charlie's Diner in Fall River with Tulio Gasparini, an excellent musician from Pawtucket, Tessier's Hall in Central Falls, and (whew!) many more. When talking with people who performed, whether they be singers, instrumentalists or dancers, we referred to the places that had no class by saying, "What toilet are you playing at tonight?" Money was the incentive.

Mother would be ready to go, too, when my date came to pick me up. Notice his face – not too happy. The girls faces – "What the heck?"

THE MAKING OF MANY COSTUMES

I learned to sew at an early age. Around 11 or 12 years old, I would spend summer days at the Kendall Street playground. Older teens and some mothers and grandmothers would set aside time for crafts. I discovered that I was very adept at sewing and making my own designs. We were given patterns to follow and at the end of the week there would be a contest to see who had made the prettiest and the best piece of clothing. I always enjoyed a challenge, so this set me free to experiment and, hopefully, win a small prize. I would borrow a sleeve from one pattern, a bodice from another, and VOILA! I had learned how to creatively design my own costumes for my future students.

When I had my own studios, I designed ALL my costumes and found a wonderful dressmaker, Barbara Chiccofiglio, who could follow my sketches to a tee. I would go to New York alone (I was very fearless) and find the best and the least expensive places that sold material. I would take the train from Central Falls to Boston to make good business sense purchases. The most ornate costumes were the ones I designed myself. I was a fan of lots of cloth, feathers and long trains flowing behind me.

I, also, found a mill in Woonsocket that sold material. From going there so often, I became friendly with the man who owned the store. He would set aside some cloth if it had a line down the middle or some other defect, yet was wearable, knowing I could use it somehow. This would save me money. My first Can-Can costume that I designed was made out of marabou feathers and fur from a store on Roosevelt Avenue in Pawtucket. The owner was a woman who sold mainly marabou and satin. I even made a dress for my daughter, Susan, from a curtain. Saving money was my goal. I had to pay the dressmaker and buy the material, but I never had an outstanding bill. My students had to buy their costumes, of course. When magazines came out with costumes in them, they had a list of what to charge. This is how I made some money. I had to make a profit somehow.

Along with taking some classes in drama and the making of backdrops and design, some examples of ways to get ideas for costumes came from movies. I would watch movie after movie to see what was worn in the past. My 1776 costumes for the 200 year anniversary at the Pawtucket Armory came from a movie. I had to change the pants look for the girls and design skirts. Another design came from one of my trips to Paris. I came home with an idea for the girls to wear an elastic fabric that covered their skin and added feathers and Swarovski crystals to the front of the material. I had 12 girls walking down stairs that my father made for me – steps in front and steps on the sides. The curtain opened and the girls walked down, two at a time.

At one of the shows, my mother noticed that some people were walking around with a pad and pencil in hand, copying my designs on paper. She exclaimed, "They're taking your ideas!" I answered, "What can I do? I can't take the pen out of their hands." There was no such thing as a copyright back then.

Joyce Davenport was 5 years old and at my first studio when she wore this costume.

In 1945 I sketched these costumes for Eileen O'Neill, Joyce Davenport, and Marion Munso.

Sarah Lussier, who was my little Shirley Temple, teaches in New York.

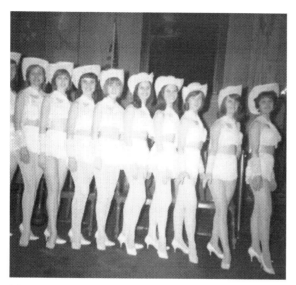

My line of girls in 1965.

1776 costumes for Pawtucket Armory's 200th anniversary.

HAPPY, HAPPY BIRTHDAY, BABIES

There was a very popular car dealership in Pawtucket owned by a man named B.A. Dario. Everyone knew that he had done very well over the years selling cars, and I had an idea for a television program but needed money and a sponsor. Once again, I went local. I thought for sure he would jump at the chance to be part of my venture when he heard me say, "I can sell your Buicks on TV!" For a week, I would leave the studio, go straight to the dealership and wait outside his office. Finally, one night he opened the door and said, "Are you STILL here?" I told him my idea of a 7:00 p.m. program on Sunday nights called "The Birthday Party." About ten children with birthday hats on would come out of a car onto a small stage. The goal was to get children whom I knew had never had a party for their birthdays to actually have one on TV, cake and all. I wanted them to have their own special time.

Somehow I sold Mr. Dario on the idea. I think it was when I mentioned that the car on the set would, naturally, be a Buick on its way to a party at 10 Buick Street. I got my father involved. He made a giant cake in a half moon shape out of wood which had three tiers that the boys and girls sat on. They wore their hats, sang songs, played games, were introduced one by one and had a wonderful birthday celebration.

The show was a success. Soon, other sponsors jumped on the bandwagon. I asked the owner of Salois Dairy if he would be interested. He said that the only requirement he had was that the kids sing a song based on the company's dairy products. We got together, made a song up really fast and the children sang to the sounds of cows and chickens. New York Lace, a popular clothing store in Pawtucket, had Susan model their latest children's line of clothes. And Bert Finberg, a local lawyer, enjoyed writing commercials and songs as a pastime. At 5 years old, Susan would memorize all the lines before show time and recite them before the camera. Walt Bischoff was the cameraman. He worked at the cable network, then move to Channel 12, as did "The Birthday Party." The studio was located in Rehoboth.

The fun lasted for a full year. A man approached Mr. Dario with a more lucrative deal for a show which would air later at night and interest the public in buying cars more so than at the earlier time. I, personally, did not make any money from the show, but it had a good run, attracted more students to the studio as a result and made a lot of kids happy.

The Happy Birthday TV show with eight little cuties getting presents. On the right is the large cake my dad made.

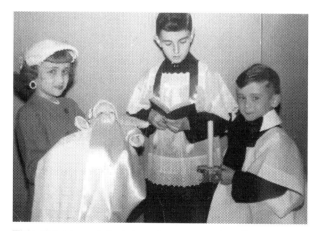

This skit on my television show was a baptism performed by "priestly" Billy Menard.

People who worked at the studio would be dressed like the sponsor. In this case, the "Salois Dairy Man" spoke with Susan, Elaine Bussey, Richard Raposa, and Eddie Badessa.

THERESA'S THE NAME, SHOWCASING'S THE GAME

Life took my students on many more journeys. My piano player at the time, Bill Sheverini, told me he had lots of friends in New York who could help me get my girls on television. After calling nearly every day, leaving several phone messages and/or asking exactly WHEN he was going to get the girls on "The Ted Mack Show," Bill must have gotten sick of my phone voice and gave me Ted Mack's address. I was so excited for the girls, as we went to the next level of popularity. I brought my high kicking line to audition for the show. They performed "The Gun Dance" and won in their category. After that, I became friendly with the talent scout manager who would call regularly and say, "I trust you, Theresa. Send me an act." There were at least ten times that I sent dancers to him, boys and girls. They always did very well; it made my heart swell with pride to watch them.

Once, while we were in New York for Ted Mack's show, Johnny Carson was working at his desk with the door open and saw me walking by with the girls. "What do you do?" he asked. I jumped at the opportunity to begin talking about my studio and my students but was told he did not have enough time to have the dancers on "The Tonight Show;" however, he would let me come on and sing a foolish ditty I had learned when I was young, plus get a plug in about the girls being on Ted's show. I was what he called a "fill-in." So I sang my ridiculous ditty, "I'm Nuts About Mutts" (a dog), but only after Johnny introduced me as a dance teacher/choreographer who had a studio in Pawtucket, RI. This time, my students said they were proud of me and of being a part of "The Theresa Landry Dancers." Later, I realized that Fidel Castro was on the show that night, and I didn't even know who he was.

For at least 12 years, every summer we were asked to dance at the Vaudeville Show on the Atlantic City Boardwalk. The producer, Tony Grant, had seen the girls on TV and had called me to audition. Once he saw the line in person, he loved it, and we were booked. The girls' parents would save their money all year and make a vacation out of it. I didn't go every year because of teaching, but when I did I would bring my daughter along. It was a fun family time. There was no pay involved; exposure was the reward.

I had a student for years, Kim Audette, who became one of my teachers and a good friend until the studio closed in 2014. Her main job was at Memorial Hospital in Pawtucket. Knowing me so well, she would ask if some of the girls could go to the hospital to perform for the patients in the rehab unit. Kim had learned well. It's all about the smiles you get in return.

One of the featured television shows on which the dancers did very well was "Community Auditions" which was filmed in Boston. My acts won often and were happy not to have to travel too far from home. It wasn't easy getting rides and having to raise money to go to New York or New Jersey. Another close to home show was on Channel 12, featuring the locally famous Salty Brine. My goal was to keep trying to open as many doors as I could. I knew the talent scouts and managers would not come to me, so I was determined to go to them as often as possible. Another philosophy of mine and what I try to relay to others is "Always keep trying."

All the while, I refused to give up on my own knowledge of new dance steps. Dance routines change just as the popularity of songs and their meanings do. I kept abreast of this fact as I traveled to the Carnegie Building in New York every week for lessons. I took castanet and tango lessons from Jose Greco on Monday nights, taking the train from Central Falls to Penn Station, then walking to 3rd Avenue. My students were never behind the times. Also, I hoped that this would encourage them to want to learn more for themselves.

These costumes were designed as a result of the first man having landed on the moon – 1969. The moon headpieces are enhanced by beaded tassles.

The gun dance costume was a popular one. The fish net stockings
and the mesh between the top and the skirt made it unique.

TRAVEL WITH SUSAN

Mothers have a tendency to live vicariously through their daughters. Once I gave birth to my beautiful daughter, I devoted my life to do for and with her what I loved so much – travel. I was still taking those weekend jaunts to Newport, but for different reasons. I would pack Susan's and my clothes, she would get her dolls and pack whatever she needed for them and off we would go to Castle Hill. I rented a huge room overlooking the water which made me feel peaceful. Then I would get to work on formatting the Play Bill for my yearly recital. I put a lot of effort into this project to make sure names were spelled correctly, certain dance numbers followed in the correct order which was important for costume changes, intermission occurred at the right time, and the list went on and on until perfection was reached. Such a time-consuming project required a lot of thought, and I could always rely upon Susan to be my best little helper in that area. I would explain that I couldn't be interrupted. She would set up her dolls and everything that she had brought for them, and I wouldn't hear a peep out of her for hours. When I saw how self-disciplined Susan was at the age of 5, I knew I had a wonderful traveling daughter companion to take on many trips.

And travel we did! A few years later, I booked a cruise for us on The Queen Mary. My mother and father drove us to Boston where we boarded. Frugality was always a part of every journey, so I could only afford a small room in the lowest of the lower level of the ship. Two bunk beds, a sink and a toilet were the only amenities in the room. We, also, had to book "shower time." The shower room was in the hall. We learned never to be late after the nasty stares we encountered from the other bookers.

We never stayed in the room too long, only to sleep and change our clothing. We saw the best shows every night and stayed on deck during the day. I found out that Fred Astaire, one of my favorite dancers of all time, and Rev. Oral Roberts and his son were staying on the upper deck in first class rooms, of course. I took Susan upstairs, and we "accidentally" lost our way. I just wanted to get a sneak peek at the stars having dinner. We managed to get a quick look before one of the crew realized we were not first class people. We had to retreat downstairs, happy anyway to have seen what and who were on the "other side."

I used to close the studio back then for one month in the summer. One of our biggest trips was when Susan was ten. I went through Caravan Tours. We visited 21 countries in 27 days. Susan remembers being on the bus a lot and hopping off to see each country's most noted monuments and key sights. She also remembers docking in Cherboug, France and staying in Paris, as well. While in Paris, I bought some cloth so we could have matching dresses which I sewed in the hotel room.

In one of the countries we visited, a man came up to me and said he wished he had a daughter like Susan to take on vacation. She was so well behaved. Part of this was due to her education which, like mine, took place in Catholic schools. She attended Mercymount Country Day School in Cumberland from the age of 5 until the eighth grade. Upon graduation, she attended St. Claire's in Woonsocket and boarded there for all of a few weeks. Being away from home was not for her, so I transferred her to St. Mathieu's (my alma mater) for the ninth grade, then St. Mary's Academy – Bay View until the end of grade 12.

I loved playing with Susan at the beach.

Susan with her dolls in Newport while I worked on my play bill.

Our friend, Ann, came to Portugal with me and Susan in 1962.

SUSIE'S EDUCATION CONTINUED

Susan continued her education at Marymount College in Boca Raton, Florida, a two year college at the time. I didn't want her to feel like she had always had to be home taking care of her father who had set the house on fire twice, once when he was home cooking steak on the stove and once when he fell asleep on the couch, with his satin pajamas on (a material which ignites quickly), and he dropped the cigarette he was smoking. I walked in the door just in time before his clothes burst into flames. I was always trying to "cure" Joe; now I realize how impossible a thought that is. I even believed in my heart of hearts that traveling might help him. The three of us went on a trip to Paris, Italy, Portugal, England and Scotland. When I opened Joe's bag to unpack for him, it was full of pills. He had started mixing drugs with the alcohol. I felt that Susan deserved to be away from these sights that had been occurring throughout her life.

Forgive me, for I digress. I knew that college in Florida was going to be expensive, so I devised a plan for Susan to come home for the holidays and summers by plane. In all my frugality, I figured that since she was only going to be 17 when school started in September, and since the rule was that up to age 16, one could fly at a lower rate, I told her she would have to "bind her bust" and put her hair in pigtails. Susan's answer was, "Oh, MOM!" But Susan did what she was told, as usual. As a graduation gift, since she often said she wanted to go and see where Jesus walked, I booked her a 52 day trip to Israel and Greece. I realized afterward that it was too long for her, and she was homesick at times, but she did appreciate the different cultures. She even worked in a kibbutz in Israel. Her tales of this make people laugh to this day.

The remainder of Susan's education was completed at Rhode Island College where she acquired a bachelor's degree in psychology. My "little girl" was married in 1972 and had my two grandchildren, Justin and Marisa, who are also the loves in my life. Unfortunately, Susan's marriage ended in divorce. I immediately went into overdrive and offered her a job teaching dance at the studio with me. She didn't need any references. I knew how well she danced and how good she was with the children. We were together until 1993 when she completed her master's degree in Mental Health. This made her marketable as a clinician/therapist, the field in which she is still working 20 years later. Justin is in the banking industry, and he and Michelle are parents to Michael, and Marissa is a CNA currently attending school to become an occupational therapist. She and Tom have a son, 5 year old Alexander.

I would be remiss if I did not mention my older sister, Irene, who passed away at the age of 89. She had made her home in Seattle, WA for years and had a son, Hugh. She wrote a fiction book entitled "Passion in Winter." She was a scholar and a linguist who, when we were younger and I was dancing in shows, claimed I was going to "go to hell." My baby sister, Bertha, at the age of 91, lives in West Palm Beach, FL in a beautiful "living apartment." She has three sons, Tom, Dan and Bob. She lived in New York when she was younger. She was an entrepreneur in Seacliff, Long Island as a restauranteur. Each of us was lucky to have the parents that we did who encouraged us to follow our own unique and individual dreams.

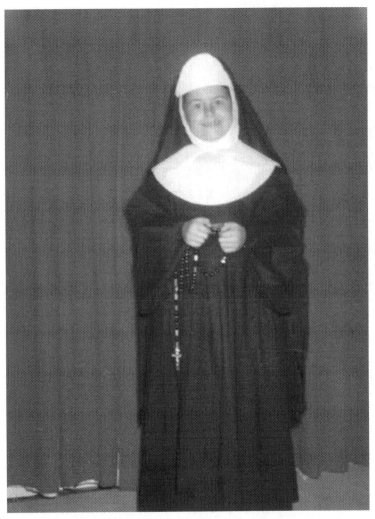

Susie said she wanted to become a nun when she
was at Mercymount. That never happened.

Myself, Irene, and Bertha – The Landry Sisters grown up.

CAN'T CURE IT

I have already alluded to my husband, Joe, however, he deserves his own vignette. Joe was an extremely intelligent man who had the plan of completing school to become a doctor after returning from the war. His family had the money to support this dream, but, by the time Joe returned, his PTSD and his alcoholism had taken control of his life. After we were married, as long as I was working, he knew he didn't have to. The bottle became his best friend on a daily basis, with short work breaks which usually ended before they began. When I would go away on one of my weekly trips, I would say, "You'd better have a job by the time I get back or that's it!" Joe knew that he could just coast along; I'd come home, go back to work, and nothing ever changed. I still hadn't learned that I could not "change" him. I'd leave with high hopes and learn that he had been found passed out in all sorts of places. Once, he walked in a drunken stupor to Lincoln Woods and was found lying on the ground. Another time when the police found him, my mother was contacted because I was in Europe. They wanted her to call me. She declined, saying, "No. I will call her only if he is dead." She knew how stressed I was over his condition.

But Joe was Joe. Kind, soft-hearted, quiet. He would even dress like Santa for the children at the studio, passing out gifts at Christmastime. Most of all, he was a loving father to Susan. When sober, he would drive her to Saint Raphael Academy's school dances and pick up her best friend, Linda, on the way. And when Susan and Linda needed help with their homework, he was the one they sought because he was so knowledgeable in math, science, English – just about any subject. And if he wasn't sure of the answer, he would look it up. The girls could count on Joe for that. Still, I felt badly that Susan had to keep up a façade about her dad. She couldn't have friends over the house or have sleepovers because we just never knew when Joe would get the urge to drink.

There was a hospital where people who had mental illnesses could go called Fuller Sanitarium on Rte.1 in South Attleboro, MA. I brought Joe there a total of fifteen times. It cost $500.00 each visit to admit him, and only cash was accepted, no checks. I was told by the staff, "You are the only wife who keeps bringing her husband in for treatment." I kept trying and trying. My other option was admitting Joe to the Veteran's Administration Hospital in Providence. There was a psychiatric ward where he could stay up to 3 months at a time. There was a doctor at the VA who said to me, "If you go out with me, I'll make sure he gets in right away all the time." I told him, "Forget it. I'll take my chances that there will be a bed for him when we come."

It got to the point that the only way for any semblance of normalcy to be in my life would come if I divorced Joe. I found him an apartment and visited him on a regular basis, bringing food, helping him to clean. All women loved talking with Joe. At an AA meeting, he met a wonderful woman named Alicia. She got an apartment above his, and they were happy together for many years. She was good for Joe. He, eventually, became wheelchair bound due to vascular problems and ulcerated feet. One day, Joe found Alicia dead on top of her bed. She had had a heart attack and not suffered. But Joe was devastated, and his health steadily declined. He died on May 11, 1999.

His was a good soul that never found its way to deal with life after his return from World War II.

In 1962, Joe and I were able to go to Paris. He
was feeling well and was happy.

Thankfully, Joe could get himself together for Susan's
graduation from Bay View in June 1966.

I had to get a shot of the woman with all the flowers atop her head.
We were in Portugal. Even on vacation, people dressed up then, Joe
in his suit and Susan and Ann with skirts, jackets, and purses.

RONNIE AND THE INFAMOUS BIKE

One night a girl came into the studio for her dance lesson and brought her boyfriend, Ronnie, with her. While she was in the class, Ronnie and I began talking. This turned into the beginning of a great relationship for both of us, even though Ronnie was in his 20's and I in my 40's. I found out that he was a handyman and hired him to do some work around the studio. For instance, I always wanted a strobe light in one of the rooms to give the students the feeling of dancing in a club-like atmosphere. Ronnie was able to do that and some much needed general maintenance work. Then I happened to hear him singing as he was working and was genuinely impressed with his talent. Afterwards, I asked him to sing at all my parties, and he really got a kick out of being in the parades in Central Falls and Pawtucket, leading the girls and dressed as a cowboy. With his longish hair and good looks, he really stood out, as he would walk up to the people and greet them, advertising the "Theresa Landry School of Dance."

Even though Ronnie was 20 years my junior, he was accepted and well-liked by my family. He became the son my father never had. Seeing his affinity in general contracting work, my father asked Ronnie if he would be interested in learning more, then my father taught him all he knew. Ronnie was grateful and loving to both my parents.

Ronnie's mother lived down in South County at Point Judith. She invited him to dinner one Saturday night, and he asked me if I wanted to go down on his motorcycle. Riding a bike like this was something I had yet to do in my lifetime, so my free spirit made me more than willing to go. On the way, as I held onto Ronnie's waist tightly, enjoying the wind blowing in my face, I suddenly developed these strange feelings that I had never experienced before, not even with my husband. Ronnie heard the heavy sounds of my voice emanating from my throat, "Ooh," "Ooh," "Ooh!" I realized that I was finally having an orgasm, a feeling I had heard other women talk about. By this time, Joe and I were divorced. What a pity that this experience had never occurred with the father of my child. Actually, I had been able to obtain an annulment, as ruled by the church, due to the life that we had led.

Time passed and my relationship with Ronnie continued to flourish. I told him that with the kind of voice he had, he needed to branch out of Pawtucket and try to get someone famous to hear him. I was due for some time off. "Want to go to Las Vegas?" I asked. And off we drove in my baby blue Cadillac convertible. We stopped at a saloon and my face lit up when I saw Loretta Lynn sitting at a table. I walked right up to her, introduced myself, and told her how well Ronnie sang. "If he sings as good as he looks, he'll go far," was her response. She was grinning from ear to ear. But I was disappointed that Loretta didn't ask him to sing right then and there. Then he wouldn't have had time to get nervous. However, I was not about to give up.

The next day, Ronnie and I took a ride by Johnny Cash's house. It looked like a large white palace surrounded by miles of plush green velvet that you could sink your toes in and feel as if you were walking on clouds. His and his wife's (June Carter) daughter was getting married that day. Because we were in my Cadillac and Ronnie was wearing his cowboy hat, the man at the gate automatically thought we were invited guests and let us in. I found out later that this man was Johnny's cell mate in prison, and when he had been released, Johnny gave him this job.

I saw Johnny on the veranda, all dressed in black, even wearing a holster and gun. He heard me explaining that I was there as a fan, hoping that I could ask Mr. Cash to listen to my friend sing. Fortunately, Johnny saw humor in this crazy woman and told us we could come into his studio right then. Ronnie was great when he sang at home, but he had very little confidence in himself. When he started to sing, he froze. Johnny was kind and said that he was sorry, but if he couldn't hear him, there was nothing he could do. After a big "Thank You," we were off, disappointed, but still excited about the experience.

Ronnie met more of my family when we took a trip to Nova Scotia. Everyone there fell in love with him, too, and why not? He was young, luscious to look at and fun to be around. Ronnie was also immature back then, a quality that was probably due to his age. At this point, I realized that my age was going up while he had much more youth to live. We had had five fun-filled years together, and Ronnie claimed that they were the best of his life up until that point. I realized that I was a lonely, recently divorced woman when I had met him, and he was young and having a great time driving my cars and going places he never would have gone to on his own. We definitely had "different perspectives" at that particular time of our lives. And it was okay. We had a mutual parting of the ways. Ronnie met a girl whom he married, and I met my Anthony. Things worked out for both of us.

Ronnie loved being on stage. He would play the
guitar as background music for a student.

TRAVEL WITH ANTHONY

"Travel with Anthony" is more like a series of vignettes beginning with our meeting and ending with a solo grieving trip after his death. Allow me to begin at the beginning of finally finding the "Love of my Life."

On most Fridays, after a late night at the studio, I would shut the lights and look forward to going to Gregg's on North Main Street in Providence with anyone who wanted to grab a bite to eat. One particular Friday night in 1991, my friend, Dorothy, and I headed for the restaurant. I was craving coffee and chocolate "anything." We were sitting on the Pub side when two men came in. Both were rather nice looking, but the one with the salt and pepper hair had a smile that immediately lured me in. Dorothy was complaining of a terrible headache when Mr. Smile stood up and said he would go to the pharmacy and get her some aspirin. After introducing himself, Anthony was off on his mission. How many men would do that for a person they don't even know? When Anthony returned, we found out that he and his friend were on their way to a convention in New York. They had an hour to wait before the bus left, so they had come to Gregg's to waste some time.

Anthony called me the very next night. I'm sure I had given him my card (Wink! Wink!). He was at The Capital Grille with his friend having potato soup and asked me and Dorothy to join them. I had never been to The Capital Grille, but being the determined person that I am, I picked up Dorothy and we drove to Providence and found the Grille quite easily. It was a beautiful place, but boring and quiet. Anthony mentioned that he liked to dance (my kind of man!). I suggested we go to Bumblebee's on Hope Street because it was a real fun place with live music. Off we went. Anthony and I were in his Cadillac and Dorothy and his friend were in mine. The place was packed with many people I knew. I introduced Anthony to everyone, then we danced the night away. From that night on we became a "couple."

"Our Vacations Together" began in the form of short trips on the weekends. Anthony loved going to New York and seeing a show. My favorite then and still remains "The Rockettes." He never balked at taking me to Radio City. We also enjoyed going to Cape Cod, a place where I delighted in the scenery and the water. But Anthony had never traveled abroad. I had been to Europe quite often by this time, and I guaranteed him we would never need a guide if he ever wanted to go. In 1995, I managed to get him to agree to visit Italy. Being Italian, he was anticipating the possibility of finding some of his family.

I did some detective work and found the address of Anthony's family. We traveled to Naples to take the train into the mountains. I saw a small building with the word "Policia" on it. We walked in, and I informed the policeman we were looking for the "Varone" family. I can still hear the policeman standing there proudly saying, "I Varone!" That got us a ride to the top of the mountain where some members of Anthony's family lived. We were told that Anthony looked just like one of their brothers who had died in the war. The family kept yelling, "Frank! Frank!" Anthony felt honored to be a part of this kind, quiet and gentle family which, ironically, was the exact way one would describe Anthony. This is why I was so attracted to him that very first night we met. There was no doubt that this was his family. As we were leaving, I looked up the hill to get one last look at this magnificent mountain top. Astonished, I said to Anthony, "There's a blue truck of potatoes!" This sign was a blend of both our lives.

Another thrill on this trip was Anthony getting to see the Pope. I explained that first we had to go to the American University to get tickets for the event of being blessed by Pope John Paul II. Once inside the Basilica, it is impossible not to become overwhelmed by the beauty and the amount of marble that surrounds you. We became friendly with another couple on the tour and concluded the night having dinner with them.

Our last night in Italy was spent enjoying drinks and excellent cuisine in a small, intimate restaurant. There were two men walking around, serenading people at their tables. One was playing the accordion and the other the guitar. When their time to play came to an end, Anthony, seeing how much I was enjoying the music, paid them to stay longer. Anthony, as always, the thoughtful, gentle man.

Anthony's eyes were definitely fixated on the cross
as we knelt in front of the church in Italy.

We toasted each other at one of our favorite cozy Italian
restaurants while were being serenaded.

Theresa Landry

MY GREATEST LOVE BECAME
MY GREATEST GRIEF

Anthony and I shared our love and our passions for nine years with never an argument. One Friday night, he called and said he wasn't feeling well, but we would definitely see each other the following night. He was going to go to bed for some much needed rest. When he called on Saturday, he still wasn't any better. "No Bumblebee's, okay?" he said sadly, sounding as if he felt guilty for ruining another night for us. I told him to stay in bed, rest some more and he would feel much better in the morning. But no one can play God. Anthony was found the next morning by his friend, as he lay on the floor on the side of his bed. He had had a fatal heart attack during the night. There was never any history of heart disease in the family, and he had been feeling fine before. So, WHY???

I had made up my mind not to attend the wake or the funeral because Anthony was separated, not divorced. The marriage had been over for years, but Anthony's family, particularly his father, did not condone divorce. Also, he had children whom he loved very much, so he had moved out of the house but held true to his fatherly duties. I was pleasantly surprised when Anthony's sister called me and said, "You need closure. Come to the wake."

This was not an answer, however, to my incessant crying jags that I could not control. I was miserable and knew I had to get away. For some reason I still do not understand, I chose to fly to Cuba. I called Bob Weygand, a politician whose campaign for Attorney General I was working for at the time. He told me to go to Collette Travel Agency in Pawtucket, and I would get the correct information on going to Toronto where I could board a propeller plane. That was the best way for me to get to my destination because, at the time, you could not travel to Cuba from the United States. I hurriedly closed the studio and was at the airport the next morning on a plane to Toronto. I, then, waited for the third, and final, propeller plane to fly me the three hours to Cuba. I cried the whole time.

I stayed at the Americana Hotel which was absolutely gorgeous. I was given an elegant VIP suite which I found out later had been previously occupied by Ginger Rogers. I had the most beautiful view of the beaches I had ever seen. The girl at the desk kept seeing me crying each time I passed by. She asked why I was so sad. After I explained, she told me that her mother had been burned to death in a terrible fire, so she knew my pain. Her story humbled me and made me realize I was not alone in such a predicament. "Try to forget and have a nice vacation" were the girl's words. After our conversation, I went to every wonderful show playing in the hotel. The desk clerk even found me a guide who drove me to the "Grande Theatre" where I actually got on the stage and performed a Spanish dance with my castanets. There was actually a smile on my face in a picture that was taken.

I have to admit that it was not a good time to travel to Cuba because Americans were not welcome. However, my illogical side overpowered my logical one at that moment in time.

BEFORE MY RETURN

I started noticing things that surrounded me again. For instance, the schools in Cuba were very clean on the outside of the buildings, as were the streets and walkways. And, as I watched the children walking around the city, they were clean and well dressed. Was I starting to miss my own students?

I met a lovely Brazilian family who invited me to their home. I was never one to be afraid to strike up a conversation with anyone. I enjoyed talking to people and listening to stories about their countries. But my travels never took me to Brazil. I did notice the gorgeous suede jackets the couple were wearing. They claimed to be in Cuba on business. What kind of business I never knew nor found out.

On one of my last days in Cuba, the guide drove me to one of the country's amazing beaches. I was laying down on my blanket, eyes closed, when I heard a voice. I saw a man standing over me asking if I would hold his watch. "I would like to take a swim," he said. No problem. When he came out of the water, he laid down on the blanket much too close to me. Too soon. I got up immediately and left. My recovery had begun, but I still needed time to continue my grieving process.

I returned to Rhode Island and my love of the 6 days a week of dancing and teaching.

TRUE LOVE CAN NEVER BE ABOLISHED

After returning from Cuba, I reopened the studio, but a strange need haunted me. I didn't know what it was until I tried to find it. Through the process, I discovered that it would never be satisfied in this lifetime.

One night, I made a conscious decision to go out alone. I put on a smooth, silk dress, but did not put on any underwear. I wanted men to feel me, feel my body against them, without any material between. I drove myself to Bobby's Roller Skating Rink where a local band was playing. As I walked in, I saw a tall, good looking blonde man talking to three attractive girls. He noticed me, too, and said hello as I passed by. He wandered over to where I was standing and asked me to dance. We didn't stop dancing until the band stopped playing. He ended up following me home.

I found out that he lived in Naples, Florida and was here on vacation visiting his brother. When it was time for him to return home, he asked if I would like to visit his house. A few weeks later, I decided to take three days off and flew to Florida. I was extremely impressed when I saw this beautiful home right next to the Vanderbilt Hotel. Never in my life did I think I would be staying in such a place. It was a two bedroom condo, and Mr. Tall, Blonde and Handsome told me to use the bureau drawers in the other room to put my clothes in. Upon opening the drawers, I noticed that some woman's clothing was in them. When I confronted him, he explained that a woman shared the condo with him. Some of the time he was there, and at other times, she was. Whether or not this was true, I will never know. At this point, I didn't even care. All I was interested in was validating my own self by letting him make love to me during the time I was there.

I realized afterwards that this was the need I was missing – a man's love. But, not this man's. The entire time I was with him, I kept my eyes closed and pretended I was with Anthony. That's when I became aware of the fact that real, true love can never be replaced.

THE DIAMOND PRINCESS OR ANCHORAGE AWAY

The titles of this vignette come from my trip to Alaska in 2005. "The Diamond Princess" is certainly not a direct reference to me; it is the name of the ship I was on which docked in Anchorage where I wandered into every single one of the many shops in the city. Again, I was feeling that urge to get away just for a week. I went to the travel agency and looked at pictures that had me gasping in awe. That was all I needed! Off I went, alone, to Alaska where it rained the entire time. I didn't care, though, because I had never seen such beautiful icebergs, and the water protruding from the rocks, spraying in all directions, was like watching a rain dance in motion. Each new site made up for my usual inexpensive room. This one had a motor under the floor which made the room shake all night as if a train were coming through it. I met a woman named Joyce on this trip, and we would laugh about my "orgasmic suite."

It had been a dream of mine to eat dinner with the Captain of a ship, and since I always followed my dreams (and still do as often as possible), I had an idea. I wrote a note to the Captain relaying my wish and saying how old I was, 84 at the time, and wouldn't it be wonderful if he would be the one to grant this request. I located the bursar and asked him to deliver the note to the Captain. This was around 10:00 a.m.; by 11:00 a.m., there was a knock on my cabin door. A young woman reminding me of Julie on the television program "Loveboat" (remember that one?) who helped everyone on the ship had come to get me to meet with the Captain and his crew on the bridge. I hurriedly put on my raincoat and a little more lipstick and scooted out the door, excitedly following her all the way. I knew I was going to have to make a really good case for getting a dinner invitation. After the Captain and I met and talked about his family, my family and my life as a dance teacher, I politely told him how I would be ever so grateful to be a guest at his dinner table. The Captain informed me that the rule was that a person had to have been on five trips in order to be granted that request. Trying to smooth this fact over, he said, "And you are way too young to have done that." Well, I must have had my hair colored just the right shade before leaving home because as we were walking back to my room, "Julie" handed me an envelope with an invitation in it to the Captain's Dinner that evening. Needless to say, I was more than jubilant. I had a wonderful time talking with all the people I met that night and made sure I shone like a star. There is a picture of me at the "Champagne Waterfall," helping to pour champagne into the top glass as it flowed down the tower of glasses beneath.

This trip was certainly one to remember. There were shows every night at 10 o'clock, and I was at every one of them. I met Russian dance teachers who were extremely strict with their students, always stressing perfection. There was even a time during the day when men and women who were interested in meeting others for companionship would get together. I went once. There were 8 women and 1 man. Great odds for HIM!

But all good trips must come to an end. I had asked for a wheelchair when I got on the ship since there were three thousand people boarding. The line was so long because you had to show your passport, and I knew that the chair would get me on much faster. People who saw me getting wheeled up to the front, then saw me dancing every night all week made comments such as, "Guess you're all better" in a sarcastic tone. That did not stop me from asking for a wheelchair when we were getting off the ship, as well. I deserved a rest. After all, the next day I was going back to work!

Even in the rain, I loved every minute of Alaska. Look at that background!

What a night. 84 years old and having dinner at the Captain's table.

I was elated to be asked to help pour the champagne. It
was even better after when I got to taste some!

THE IMPORTANCE OF GIVING BACK
OR
RAZZLE DAZZLE

Besides always wanting my students to be seen as the rising stars they were and boosting their self-confidence, I also valued the importance of giving back to the community. I considered myself lucky and had made my own luck over the years. I had met the right people at the most opportune times, found the best places to use as my studios and was rewarded time and again with great students who were my best advertisements for my school. My good fortune made me want to give back for all I had received, so I performed in various locations around Rhode Island for free for people who would benefit through the enjoyment of seeing a show with children tap dancing, gracefully ballet dancing, moving to music and performing fantastic acrobatic feats.

My most favorite place to put on a show was at the Jeanne Jugan Residence on Main Street in Pawtucket run by the Little Sisters of the Poor. We would perform there four times a year. The women enjoyed the performances so much, and the Sisters were always grateful. Of course, the biggest hit of the shows were the "babies." Who doesn't love little sweeties, 2, 3 and 4 years old, moving their tiny feet and tushies while blowing kisses? The women would laugh, cry and sing to the music as these darlings danced. I'm sure each elderly person allowed a favorite memory to slip into her mind during these times. I made it mandatory that each student bring a small gift to the Home. At the end, they would bring their gifts up to the ladies in the audience. It was heartwarming to watch the faces of both the younger and the older generations coming together as one.

Performances at the Saint Aloysius Home were enjoyed by many, as well as those at The Veterans' Hospital. The holidays were lonely times for many who had no families, and any glimmer of joy was much appreciated. I was extremely partial to going and seeing the staff and the people who were at Rose's Cottage in Central Falls during this time where my students had shone their talents quite often, since this was the place where my mother had spent her last days. The smiles on the patients' faces at all of these hospitals/homes were my payment.

One particular memory stands out when we did a show at the Adult Correctional Institution in Cranston. I had been asked if my dancers would perform for the inmates, and my piano player at the time, Bill Sheverini, was a nervous wreck when I told him. He did not want to play while prisoners were all around him. Finally, he, begrudgingly, gave in. Before the show began, it just so happened that I needed to cut some threads from one of my girl's costume. Not thinking of where we were, I placed the scissors down right on top of the baby grand piano at which Bill was sitting. He jumped up to run out the door when about ten security guards rushed down to grab the potentially dangerous "weapon." I learned a very important lesson and received a harsh scolding from the senior guard. Yet, I must admit that Bill's face was worth a thousand words, all angrily directed at me!

At the Pawtucket Armory building on Exchange Street, my girls danced for the 200 years celebration of the War of 1776 in 1996. I was so proud. I actually went to Boston to see the movie about the war so I recreate and design the costumes for this show. My girls also represented Rhode Island at the Expo in Montreal in soldier uniforms. Again, I had to redesign the costumes with a mesh material so they could move freely to do the dance movements. Then I was asked to send 8 girls to the Texas EXPO. I flew down to set the music with a 16 piece orchestra but couldn't stay because I had to come home to teach. One of my girl's mothers offered to chaperone. I knew she would take good care of these young ladies, so I wasn't worried. This was an actual paying job. We received $2500.00 which I split evenly among the girls. They were ecstatic and I was proud.

It was wonderful for these kids to be able to perform on any of these stages and hear the applause. Plus, there were some great success stories that came from the confidence that these young people acquired. For example, one of my students, Chris Smith, made it big in Nashville and returned to thank me. She had grown up in Fall River. Her mother had heard of my studio and how much the students learned and loved dancing there. The mother drove her to the studio for lessons from the age of 6, and it was well worth it since her future was determined for all her work and her mother's unselfish act.

These are the special moments in my life. Everything was done to showcase the students.

Bertha Dusault was living in this home when I visited with my students. The flowers I brought were to celebrate her 105th birthday.

Ronnie's mother was residing at The Jeanne Jugan Home
when we performed there once. I made sure I gave her a
big hug. We had known each other so long by then.

People in the nursing homes love the babies.

Everything, a tug on the ear, a move left or right, makes people smile.

The Christmas show at Slater Park is always a hit.
Who can resist Santa and the Mrs.?

Every student receives a comment and their names are
said loud and clear. Here are Alexion and Jean!

July 4, 2014 at the Pawsox game at McCoy Stadium. I was asked
to provide the entertainment. The students were thrilled.

It is obvious how short I am standing next to this
beautiful girl modeling my costume.

Meredith Butter came along to show off the 1776 costume at the game.

When asked to do something my students never say no! Batter up!

MI BEACH CASA: A LITTLE BIT OF HEAVEN

After having gone down to Ronnie's mother's beach house so often for Sunday dinners and sometimes staying overnight in the bedroom that had bunk beds, I soon realized how much I loved being at the ocean, watching the sun dancing on top of the water. And the sunsets were...I can't think of any word that does them justice, except "breathtaking." There was a small house (almost the size of a big box) right on the main road at Breakwater Village. I knew I just had to have it.

I walked over to introduce myself to the owners. The man said he and his wife were from Woonsocket. He was eating his dinner and told me to come back later. When I returned, I found out that the wife was very ill. He explained that he would sell the house, but the land was considered leased at that time. That very night he agreed to sell me my dream "casa" for $3600.00. I ran home and quickly called my sister, Bertha, asking her to go in half with me since I didn't have the entire amount to give right then. I knew she loved the ocean as much as I and figured we could be together when she came to visit my mother. She agreed.

Once, when she was at the beach house, Bertha went out dancing one night. There was a place called The Dutch Inn that had good bands. She came back to the house with a man she had been dancing with and found an old dishpan in the cupboard so he could soak his feet. She had worn the poor guy out. I guess one could tell we were sisters. Always on the go. I said, "Bertha, you just met him and you're letting him soak his feet in our dishpan?" She answered, "Well, after dancing all night, we're more than just friends." Okay!

Bertha tired of the beach house. She really didn't get to utilize it that often, only when she would come from New York to visit my mother. When I decided I wanted to extend the small box house and add a porch in the front and a closet in the back, Bertha told me to buy her out for $1800.00, the amount she had originally invested. She had found a lake house in New Hampshire that her three sons liked a lot better and had decided to buy it. We were both satisfied with this deal.

I was making enough money to pay the taxes and soon put on the two additions which made the house look so much bigger and fancier. I never rented the house the entire time my mother was alive. She loved driving down with me and staying for a week or so, and I never knew when I would have the extra time which made it handy that the house was always available.

Bertha still came to visit. She and my mother had gone to the beach house on one of her trips home while I stayed behind to run the studio. My father was working at Kendall Street School doing some construction work. I got worried because I hadn't heard from him in 3 or 4 days. I had an unlisted phone number and thought maybe he had forgotten it. But why wouldn't he have dropped by the house or the studio? Pops was a Central Falls City Councilman. Four days earlier he had gone to a council meeting, then out to dinner with friends. He had an enjoyable evening, everyone said. But it would be his last. When I walked into his home, calling his name and running from room to room, I found him face down in the bathroom. He had had a fatal heart attack. Ironically, my father had previously told me that every morning he prayed that he and my mother would pass from this world quickly, without pain. The doctor comforted me by saying that my father's prayers were answered that night.

My mother came to live with me in my house in Central Falls when she was 81 until she reached the age of 90. When she passed away, I began adding on to the beach house even more. When the real estate owners began selling the land, I was the first to buy. The house is considered ocean front on elevated land. If I had an extra $50 dollars one week, I would buy some planks to be delivered until there were enough to build a bigger screened-in porch. Later, I replaced the screens with sliding windows. There was a group of men who lived in the area and they would go around looking for odd jobs to do for the residents. They referred to themselves as "The Hell's Angels," and for food and beer they built me a gorgeous deck on top of the house from which, on a clear day, anyone standing up there can see Block Island. It's also fantastic for watching the boats passing by and the beautiful sunsets. What is seen is a true gem of many colors.

I decided to start renting the cottage. No one went there anymore on a weekly basis, and other renters were telling me how much money they were charging that I could easily get, also. I began renting for $750.00 a week. Currently, I am replacing the shingles on the outside. I never stop with the upkeep, something I learned from my father. I have recurring renters every year who know where to go to sightsee, which restaurants they like best, and all they have to do to get to the ocean is cross the tiny street and descend the newly built stairs. The rent is now $1700.00 per week during prime time, July and August, and $1400.00 per week in June, September and October. I still go down every Sunday to change the sheets which I wash and iron myself and clean the entire house. I have the help of Susan, of course, and my grandchildren, as well. It keeps me young.

Up until 2 years ago, when I was working, I would go to the beach house for one week before rental season began and one week in the fall. Now I go for 1 or 2 nights, just to relax, go up on the deck, look at Block Island in the distance and watch the sunbeams dance on the water.

This is a photo of the summer house with all the additions. My license plate reads "FAME."

Two years ago, I was still driving to the beach house. Here I am loving my car right on the corner of Lane 1 where the house is. I kept my "FAME" plate.

OH, THE MEN IN MY LIFE!

MY LITTLE FRED ASTAIRE

Anyone who grew up in my generation and went to the movies, as did everyone I knew on Saturday afternoons, saw many films featuring Fred Astaire. Hat and cane in hand, dancing so smoothly across the screen, he made it appear as if he were gliding on ice. The star had a remarkable talent. This same innate talent was obvious in my 12 year old student, Rèjean Duprè. Rèjean was tall and thin, the perfect stature for a tap dancer. He was my little Fred Astaire in many shows during the six years he took lessons. After high school, Rèjean found his niche in hairdressing. Even though he left the studio, he would always come by to visit as often as he could. He opened a salon which quickly became extremely popular. Whenever I would see him walking down the street, he looked like a movie star. I can still envision him in his long white coat, dashingly handsome.

Eventually, Rèjean moved to Florida where his new salon flourished. He became friendly with a woman 20 years his senior. Their friendship grew into a beautiful love for each other. Next thing I knew, I received an invitation to their wedding. I wouldn't have missed it for the world. Their home was like something out of a magazine with one elevator going into the house and one going up to the bedrooms. It was a Floridian mansion. After a number of years together, Rèjean's wife's health began to fail. He never neglected her. He was at her side every day, all day, until the very end.

Rèjean visits Rhode Island 3 or 4 times a year. When he calls to say that he is on his way, I look forward to being treated like a queen. He picks me up in style in his Maserati convertible, and we drive to Capriccio's in Providence and dine on excellent cuisine. He even introduced me to a new love the last time he was in town – champagne! As soon as I know he is on his way to Rhode Island, I get my hair and nails done, dress in my finest garb, and sip my glass of bubbly as Rèjean tells me how much I have meant to him all these years. Ah-h-h-h-h-h-.....

Rèjean treats me like a queen wherever we go.
Here he is spoiling me, as usual.

MY SMILING IRISH SON

His mother taught him Irish step dancing from the time he was big enough to hold onto the kitchen sink. She was wise to tell him that he had to learn American tap dancing, as well. It was evident that he was going to be a star at that early an age.

Allow me the honor of introducing you to the recipient of the 2014 National Endowment of the Arts National Heritage Fellowship, Mr. Kevin Doyle!

Kevin began taking lessons from me at the age of 10. He had been to Ireland where he performed as a step dancer, and he knew how to exude true showmanship without being a showoff. When a student took lessons at the studio, I gave him or her a junior diploma after 8 years and a senior diploma after 10, both of which Kevin earned.

I would always try to open a show with an act with Kevin in it. His smiling Irish eyes combined with the smile on his face never failed to wrap the audience around his little finger right away, as everyone reviewed their playbill to see the name of this adorable little boy. One year, Kevin was in the opening of the recital at the Veteran's Auditorium in Providence with twenty other young boys, including Fr. Joseph Paquette, retired pastor and good friend from St. Theresa's Church on Newport Avenue in Pawtucket. The boys were dressed as newsboys with caps on, walking in from the back of the auditorium. Each boy was holding newspapers as they yelled, "EXTRA! EXTRA! Read all about it! Theresa Landry is having an EXTRAVAGANZA tonight!" When they arrived on the stage, the boys would all begin their dance which would lead into Kevin's solo performance.

Kevin's solos were always greatly anticipated by the audience. One particular favorite was his impersonation of Pat Rooney. Kevin would dance what was called "group work" which included the hat and cane, soft shoe, buck, then buck and wing, rhythm, double rhythm and mitting tap rolls. He could do them all and never miss a step or a beat. Kevin would impersonate dancers from different countries, for example, France or Spain, and innately know the ways in which their dance routines differed from each other.

All too soon, for me that is, Kevin had to leave the studio to obtain a full time job. Shortly after, he met the love of his life, Donna, married and had children. His daughter step dances with him in some of the shows he does, as well as his sister. Kevin has been a part of the group called "Pendragon" since 1996. They perform at The Blackstone River Theatre and throughout New England. Also, he can be seen playing various instruments and dancing with the Atwater and Donnelly husband and wife duo. At every event I attend, he introduces me and mentions how he began dancing at my studio.

Kevin has remained by my side all these years. When the building my studio was in was sold and I decided to retire, there he was among the helpers, taking pictures down (oh, so many), taking equipment apart, packing boxes, anything he could do to be of service. He and his wife still pick me up regularly to go to dinner at Kay's in Woonsocket, knowing how much I love their lobster rolls. And just recently, I needed some cream for my legs, and Kevin's wife, a nurse, knew just what to bring me.

When Kevin was awarded the National Endowment of the Arts National Heritage Fellowship, I was not surprised. I was surprised when he came to the house with papers in hand that read, "Kevin Doyle requests the pleasure of the company of Ms. Theresa Landry-Stevenson..." I was Kevin's guest at the National Endowment Awards for three days in Washington. The first day was the Library of Congress ceremony followed by a banquet; day two was a show at the Library of Congress then a party at the Irish Embassy; and day three included a visit to the Capital in the morning and a performance at the Lisner Auditorium at night. Phenomenal! Best of all was that Kevin had everything prepared for me from plane tickets to a gorgeous hotel room. And he introduced me at every venue. This award is the highest a dancer can get. How fortunate I was to be able to see Kevin achieve this honor.

As I watched Kevin perform in Washington and as I attend as many of his shows as I can to this day, my mind takes me back to all the talent shows Kevin was in, his dancing at the Jeanne Juggan Residence, at Martino's, Murphy's Lounge and the Stardust Lounge at night and coming in 1st place the very first time I sent him to "The Ted Mack Show."

Kevin and I have remained friends all these years. I still bring him flowers whenever I go to his shows, and he still introduces me, as I stand proudly and blow him a kiss. I am blessed.

This picture was taken when Kevin received
his National Award in Washington.

DEAR, DEAR JOHN

There was a family who owned a beach house in the back of the one owned by Ronnie's mother. The couple had 3 children, 2 boys and a girl. The husband, John, would see me pull up in the convertible and bust his wife up by saying how he would love to go for a ride with the woman who owned that car. I learned this from John later on. A year or so went by, and I heard that John's wife had died suddenly during the off season. Sometime later, after politely waving and/or saying "Hi" to each other, John sent the boys over one night to invite me out to dinner. "My daddy thought it would be nice to have a woman at the table," one of the boys said. Mother was with me that week at the house and told me to go. "What harm could there be in that?" John kept asking me out, and we became a couple who totally enjoyed each other's company.

John was a quiet and conservative man. After his wife died, his mother told him to sell the house and go live with her. That way, she could take care of the children while he worked. It was the best solution for all. When I asked John to attend my sister's wedding with me in New York, his mother was able to be with the children without any disruption. All the ladies loved him at the wedding. He was a dark haired, tanned Italian, suave and attractive. John had never traveled outside of the U.S. I guess I attracted this type of man more often than I thought. Maybe they thought that with me they would find adventure! And John did. Together we went to England, Scotland and Paris. Thank goodness he had moved in with his mother.

Teknor Apex, a company located in Pawtucket, is where John worked for 25 years. There was going to be a dinner, and John was receiving some type of award for his tenure there. I told him he needed a little sprucing up. We went shopping for a nice suit, and I specifically gave the order, "No white socks." We worked well as a couple, helping each other in things we knew about. He was a wonderful help with my book work and with my mother. If I had late rehearsals or Sunday shows, he would stay with her so I wouldn't worry. I'm not so sure that his mother appreciated it when I gave him a perm, but he sure looked sexy. I would tell him he was MY Burt Reynolds.

John asked me, repeatedly, to marry him. But, I said, "No, it wouldn't be fair. I work all day and can't take care of your children." Finally, we were at The German Club one night, dancing, when a woman starting coming on to John quite obviously all night long. This kept going on for a few weeks. She had a white Cadillac and would ask him to polish it for her. Soon he was gone from me, thinking of greener pastures. After a brief tryst with the woman, John came to my door, begging forgiveness. I refused, saying, "No. Once someone does that, he will do it again." Sadly, I ran into that woman one night, and she told me that she really never had any feelings for John. She just wanted to prove that she could take him away from me. Even sadder was the fact that, shortly after, John died of a heart attack at age 47.

We had a wonderful time the night of the Apex banquet. I loved John's perm.

Theresa Landry

MY ACE OF HEARTS

Ace grew up in Central Falls. He was part of the Liberty Street Boys back in the day, a bunch of really nice guys who loved to play baseball, football and go ice skating on the pond down the street. Ace was a perfect gentleman and knew, at a young age, how to say the right things to the right people at the right time. No wonder his future profession as a salesman made him very successful.

What a surprise when, years later, I found out that Ace and his wife owned a small cottage diagonally in back of my summer house. When we would see each other outside, we would talk about the old days and the people we had known growing up. I was coming out of church one Sunday, and Ace was sitting in his car parked directly behind mine. I had recently found out that his wife had passed away a while back, so I offered my condolences. He asked me what I was doing that afternoon. I answered, "Going to the beach house, of course." He said that he had nothing to do and offered me a ride down. He was "lonely" and would enjoy some company. Thus, the beginning of a really good friendship and many Sunday dinners. Ace loved only the best restaurants. Nice!

In the beginning, Ace would help me out around the beach house, but when he started getting involved with the studio, he was in his glory. He was a great help to me whenever and wherever I needed him. He, especially, liked getting all dressed up in a suit with a matching shirt and tie, as he collected the tickets and the money at the recitals. He would walk around with the box of money under his arm for fear it would get stolen or lost. And I would say, "That has a lot of money in it. Have someone walk with you," fearing someone would hit him over the head for it. Ace and I watched out for each other in many ways.

Ace and his wife never had any children, so, years later, when he began getting sick, he decided to sell his house in Cumberland and move into an assisted living establishment called Emerald Bay. It was the best thing for him. He couldn't take care of himself anymore. And the people who worked there were so good to him. I had wanted to take him to my house but was dissuaded to do so because of the level of care that he needed. Yet, I felt that it was my turn to help Ace. I was still driving, so I would pick Ace up, and we go to The Newport Creamery. He loved ice cream. I told the girl who worked there that I would tip her $5.00 each time we came if she would come out to the car window and ask him what his "delight" was to be that day. She would wait patiently while he decided on a flavor. At this point, Ace was having a hard time walking, and this made him feel special. We would do this at least 3 times a week. All those years that we were together before Ace fell ill, we would go to our Sunday restaurant, have some wine and talk. Nothing more. And every Saturday, Ace would bring coffee and donuts to the studio, for me and my secretary, Kathy. He deserved his ice cream.

Two days before Ace died, he kept saying over and over, "Theresa, I love you." He had never said that to me in all the years we were together. I believe he knew he was dying and wanted me to know that he did love me and that he appreciated our time as "best friends."

Ace loved to look dapper when we went out. And I loved to dress up and wear my fur coats. We were a happy match on this particular night.

MEET MY FRIEND GERRY

At my grandson Justin's wedding, I must have said hundreds of times, "Meet my friend, Gerry," as people walked over to the table to say hello. Gerry sat between me and my youngest sister, Bertha. Lucky him!!! Two beautiful ladies on each arm all night. I'm sure he was exhausted just from hearing the two of us talking. But Gerry enjoyed the attention. Who wouldn't?

Gerry Cournoyer and his wife lived across the street from me on Shawmut Avenue from the time I moved there. When I would see his wife outside, I would walk over and chat for a while. She was a very pleasant and beautiful woman who kept a good conversation going. Gerry was the quiet one, and he knew he had a jewel for a wife.

As time has a tendency to do, it passed by much too quickly for Gerry's wife who fell ill and died. I felt bad for Gerry. I would see him solemnly walking to his car day after day, looking sad and forlorn. I decided, what the heck, all he could say was, "no." I asked him if he would like to take a drive down to the beach on Sunday. I told him how soothing and healing watching the water could be, if you would let it. From that day on, Gerry and I have been good, purely platonic car mates.

I can't count the number of times Gerry has come to the beach house to fix something, to help clean something or just to watch the water. And since a bad fall I had in 2014, he has been kind enough to hold my hand as I climbed stairs, take me to breakfast almost every morning at Maria's on Smithfield Avenue in Lincoln or to dinner at Twin's Pizza on Mineral Spring Avenue in North Providence. Gerry has also been known to cart me to my doctor's appointments, the supermarket, my accountant's office, etc., etc., etc. Of course, there are those days when Gerry just doesn't "feel like it," but we all have those, don't we?

"Oh, Gerry, could we take a quick ride to Staples?"

Gerry was sitting in my living room very patiently waiting for me
and Bertha to head out for Justin and Michele's big day.

Theresa Landry

MY RIGHT HAND KATHY

It goes without saying that when you own a business, you can't do everything all by yourself. I soon realized that as the amount of children taking lessons began increasing. I had less and less time to sit at the desk, greet everyone who came in and collect the lesson money. I hired a secretary, Judy Benevides, who was doing a great job, but she decided to return to school full time. I was telling my tale of woe to a young student of mine, Karen, when, all of a sudden, she mentioned that her sister may be interested. She brought Kathy in, and it was instant click. Kathy worked for the State of Rhode Island, but she was free on Saturdays, my busiest day. What a Godsend!

Kathy has been my best friend ever since. She ended up working for me for thirty years, right to the bitter end of cleaning everything out of the studio two years ago. She has always been there for me, whatever I need. Always reliable, always loyal. When Kathy's mother died, we had something even more in common. I think I filled in a motherly role void somehow for her, at least I would like to think that I did in order to help her go through such a painful time. If nothing else, I certainly kept her busy. When I needed a ride to the dressmaker, Kathy was available; when I had to make a run to Boston or New York, one call to Kathy, and we were on our way. And we have gone to see the Rockettes Christmas Show almost every year together, until two years ago.

For thirty years, Kathy was my main woman behind the desk as seen by every parent, student and sibling as they walked down the hallway. She was the greeter, the lesson money collector, the person to talk to about costumes, buying shoes or just how your day was going. Kathy was always there to answer questions and to listen.

Even though Kathy retired from her state job since the studio closed and found another one to keep her active self busy, she still finds time for me. We went downtown Pawtucket to see the filming of "American Buffalo" and met Dustin Hoffman. She picks me up on her day off and takes me shopping or to lunch or for a ride to the beach house and dinner by the water.

Kathy Zabek will always remain my "Best Pal."

Here's Kathy, enjoying the beach as much as I do.

OH, IF THE PICURES ON THOSE WALLS COULD TALK...

Every inch of space on the walls at the studio, going up the stairs, in the hall and down the hallway, was covered by a picture. There were pictures of my students, my family, my teachers, but the ones that made people stop and react with a gawk factor were those of the famous people I had met and had a photo taken with over the years. Therefore, I have decided to include a picture gallery within the pages of this book which includes many of the people and places about which I have allowed myself to reminisce. And since books are meant for those who appreciate the visual arts (like me), why not share these people, places and best of times with my new category of special people in my life, you, the readers of this book.

The stories of HOW I met some of these people are equally as interesting as the pictures. I must begin with Rhode Island's own Salty Brine ("No School Foster-Gloucester") of radio and TV, where the girls performed on his morning show. Salty lived down in South County, and when I would be at the summer house and see him in the city, he would introduce me to anyone he was with saying, "Know who this is? It's Theresa Landry," as if everyone knew me. I met and have a photo with Jose Greco, a famous dancer in New York, who was also in a movie with Ann Margaret. I took lessons from him every Monday, dancing his extremely sexy tango while r-r-r-r-r-rolling the castanets with my fingers. I would take the train from Central Falls to Penn Station, then walk to 3rd Avenue. I found out that singer Sophie Tucker was staying at the Biltmore Hotel in Providence. There was a young man working at the front desk, and I very casually asked what floor Ms. Tucker's room was on. He actually told me not only the floor, but the room number, as well! My guess is that he assumed we knew each other. I found the door and knocked. Ironically, I had the little girl with me who impersonated Ms. Tucker in the show we had just performed downstairs. She sang Ms. T's theme song, "Some one of these days." As the door opened, I introduced myself, asking if she would listen to my protégé. She did! After the girl sang, Ms. Tucker said, "Very nice," and closed the door. At least my sweetheart was seen by a bigtime professional. Always promoting!

Another picture includes Ed Sullivan, variety show host in New York. He was leaving his building and getting into his car when I ran up and asked him if my friend could take a picture of me and him. No "Shrinking Violet" am I!! There was Kate Smith, famous for her lovely rendition of "When the Moon Comes Over the Mountain," as her weekly showed ended each week and Dolly Parton, such a friendly person, whom I met at a club in Massachusetts. Tommy Tune was starring in the play "Tea for Two" in New York when I went to the show and asked to meet him. And once when I was in Las Vegas, I met Frankie Laine, Englebert Humperdink and The Four Stepbrothers. Again, I used my own dancing status and was given a special badge to wear which allowed me to sit and watch the stars entering. Later, Frankie Laine came to Rhode Island to sing at Rhodes on the Pawtuxet, then to Massachusetts at Blinstraub's. He asked me to initiate a Rhode Island fan club for him, but I explained how busy I was. He understood, or so he said. The best sport of all was Jimmy Durante who agreed right away to a picture with me at Blinstraub's in Boston. Massachusetts had a summer stock tent where I met Judy Garland. She was there for Liza Minelli's show. When I asked for an autograph, her response was, "I'm not here to give autographs. I'm here to enjoy my daughter." Well, alright then!

In 1964, Liberace was playing the piano in his own magical way at The Warwick Musical Theatre, "The Tent," as it was known. My mother absolutely adored him, but it was difficult to get her in and out of the car to see the show. I had a "Theresa" idea. I honed all my baking skills and created a cake with chocolate frosting in the shape of a baby grand piano, then used white icing to make the image of the keys on it. I drove to the Tent, and I left my mother in the car while I handed the cake to a security guard who, in turn, brought it in to show Liberace. This renowned pianist sauntered out of his dressing room, and together we walked to the car so he could meet my "Mom." He was the sweetest person to do that. Of course, I managed a picture with him while we were talking.

Another time, I was at my favorite place in Newport, Castle Hill, when I noticed actor Dennis Franz waiting in line for a hot dog. I walked up to him and said, "I know you. How about a picture of you kissing me?" He gladly obliged, and I knew that his wife was standing right beside him, so the picture on the wall of me and Dennis Franz kissing was alright with her. Afterwards, I even told his wife that he kissed very nicely and that she was a lucky woman.

I was introduced to Dustin Hoffman on the set of "American Buffalo" which was being filmed near the Pawtucket Post Office. He looked at me and asked, "How did you get inducted into the Pawtucket Hall of Fame?" I guess I just happened to mention that fact to him. I went on to explain the rules about having to be acknowledged for what I had done for the city of Pawtucket. First, the person has to be nominated and letters have to be sent to the committee by the people who endorse the candidate. A good friend and one of the mothers of a student of mine, Jeanne Corvese, had sent my name in with 52 letters that she had collected from people who felt I deserved this honor. Each person wrote regarding their feelings about the various shows I had put on for The Little Sisters of the Poor, various nursing homes in Pawtucket, the Christmas show at Slater Park and my refusal to take money for any of them. They also mentioned my dedication and love for the students. Being recognized for these acts was a highlight in my life. Dustin Hoffman was impressed. Imagine that? A movie star being impressed by ME!

One of my favorite stories about meeting famous people occurred in Paris when I was on vacation with Anthony. I had recently read an article about Christian LaCroix and Christian Dior, both incredible designers, working together on dresses for a modeling show in Paris. At the time, I was looking for something different and elegant to wear to the Hall of Fame dinner and, as usual, was trying to be frugal.

Anthony said to me, "Let's go in and pretend we're going to buy something here." I looked up and read the sign on the store front, "Christian Dior." I told Anthony that I certainly did not want to spend four thousand dollars, the going rate for a dress at this establishment. But in he guided me. We were told by a very sophisticated looking and sounding woman to sit on the oh-so-comfortable zebra print couch. The next showing of dresses began a few minutes later. Ten models paraded before us, daintily twisting and turning, showing off each ruffle and delicate fold of the dresses they were wearing. The woman informed us that it would take six weeks to fill an order. Thinking quickly, I politely answered that, unfortunately, I did not have time to wait that long as my city's Hall of Fame was to occur before that. I expressed that we were visiting from the United States and had seen that Christian LaCroix was designing there, also. I asked if it would be possible to meet him. She left and returned a short time after, saying that Monsieur LaCroix was not feeling well but would take a brief minute to say "Hello." Out he came, handkerchief covering his nose. There was not much conversation, but definitely a lot of charm from Mr. LaCroix.

I have always been a fan of politics and politicians, whether it be televised news or articles written in the daily papers (The TIMES or the PROVIDENCE JOURNAL). Whenever I have heard of any politician coming to the area, I try to meet him or her. I believe it is important to keep abreast of what is happening in our world and our state. Seeing how the politicians are handling important issues is a way for me to exercise my mind. It is always the best way to become involved in outside conversation and, at the same time, knowing what I am talking about. Staying alert is the key to longevity.

The politicians I have enjoyed meeting include, first and foremost, President John Fitzgerald Kennedy. I was driving down the street in Newport when I saw a black Cadillac convertible stopped to make a turn. I knew the area well and realized that the car was waiting to go into the driveway of the Auchinclos house, Jackie Kennedy's family's home. Naturally, I slowed down and was amazed to see President Kennedy driving and Jackie in the back seat. I stopped the car. I had an apple on the seat next to me, and the only thing I could think of was to offer it to them. As I held out my hand with the fruit in it, JFK laughed, said "Hello," and told me that they were just returning from the golf course. He shook my hand. I couldn't believe I was holding President Kennedy's hand!

When I first met Ted Kennedy, he was speaking at a small club in Central Falls. I remember it being very stuffy due to so many people being in the room. The next time I saw him was on Capitol Hill. He had remarried by then. I was with Anthony, and we were all talking about my being a dancer. Ted said, "Theresa, show off those dance legs. Vickie, did you know this lady is a dance teacher?" He was a very congenial man who remembered everything you told him. Great asset to have for the political arena.

Another hand holding I recall was with President Clinton. He was giving a speech at the Polish Club in Pawtucket. I walked up to introduce myself, and President Clinton held my hand between the two of his, very gently. What impressed me about him was his quick reaction when a little girl tripped and was falling over into the busy street. Clinton saw her and ran, scooping her up from the fall. This type of humanistic memory is the kind that will stay with me forever.

There have been local politicians that I have met in my lifetime, as well. I frequented the restaurants on Federal Hill and would often see Mayor Buddy Cianci. He was always friendly and smiling. One night, I had taken my mother out in Newport to The Black Pearl restaurant, and she saw Buddy sitting on a couch talking with a woman. She liked the mayor and asked me if I would go and tell him how much she wanted to meet him. Anything for Mom. I walked over to the couch and explained how much my mother would appreciate meeting him. Mayor Cianci bounced right up and walked straight to her. She was thrilled. He had a fan for life.

Another local politician whom I had known since he was at student at St. Raphael's Academy in Pawtucket was Bob Weygand. When he was running for office, I attended a fundraiser with Anthony, my daughter, Susan, and her friend, Linda Simoneau, at the Marriott Hotel in Providence. I had a cake made for him with his image drawn on it in different colored icing. He was grateful for the thought and support. The reason I knew Bob when he was young is because Walt Bischoff, the same who worked as a cameraman on my "Birthday Party" show in the '50s on station WNET, called me in 1965, saying he was going to produce a program which would air on Sunday nights, and he needed my help. The years had been good to Walt. He had moved to another station and had moved up the ranks in the television industry. The program was to resemble a popular teenage show, "American Bandstand," which was hosted by Dick Clark. Walt needed teenagers to dance on the show. No problem! I just happened to have a teenage daughter who coerced her friend, Linda, into being on the program (it didn't take too much coercing to be on TV), and I knew lots of students who were teens, too. I hurriedly put out feelers to St. Raphael's Academy through my male students who went to school there, and Bob was one of the boys who was interested. The name of the program was "WING DING." The kids had a lot of fun dancing to the '60s music, lip syncing and being on camera for all their friends to see. What a coincidence to meet Bob in a totally different capacity later in the political stage of his life.

Meeting each of these people was a wonderful experience, but I have saved the best and most humbling for last. During my lifetime, I have had the honor to be blessed by two Popes. Susan and I had traveled to Italy in 1959 when she was 10 years old. We were fortunate enough to go to the Vatican and be blessed by Pope John XXIII. When I went to Italy in 1995 with Anthony, it was necessary to, first, go to the Monsignor to obtain tickets. A limousine would then drive those who booked a blessing up the hill and wait until the people were ready to come down. Anthony was not a very religious person. Our picture was taken while kneeling at the altar, and when I look at it now, I see what he meant when he told me that he "felt" something that day. He called it a feeling of "serenity." In the picture, Anthony has a solemn expression on his face, but he, also, looks like he found the meaning of humility and the presence of faith. He often spoke of this moment, having been blessed by Pope John Paul II, with reverence.

I have cherished the blessings by these two Popes my entire life. They have given me a great sense of peace.

Speaking of the clergy reminds me of my own student who became a "man of the cloth." I briefly mentioned Joseph Paquette, a.k.a. "Father Joe," as a young student of mine. Whenever I think of Father Joe, all I see is the little boy who always had a big smile for me and was kind to every student in his tap class. You could tell, even when he was that young, that his would be a life dedicated to helping people, and what better way to live that life than through the church. Whenever there was something to be done, whether to be fixed or cleaned, anything, Joe would offer his services.

Last year, Susan and Linda went to England, Scotland and Wales with a group of people from St. Theresa's Church in Pawtucket where Father Joe was the former pastor prior to his retirement. He still organizes these yearly trips to Europe. The day they left was a beautiful, sunny Sunday in September. I went to see them off in the church parking lot. I brought my "boy" a bouquet of flowers (which he graciously donated to the Church) and told him to have a great trip and, most of all, keep my Susan safe. Upon their return, I learned that, just like my "boy" way back, Fr. Joe helped Susan more than he thought he would have to. It seems that there was a problem with her passport and getting through customs in Boston. So, who stayed with her to help? Father Joe. And upon their return from England, Susan and Linda's luggage was left behind at the hotel. So, who waited with them for the taxi to bring the suitcases to the airport? Father Joe. The main thing was that he did what he was told. He got them home safely.

Recently, Susan, Linda and I attended a "Father Joe Roast" at the Crowne Plaza. The roof at St. Theresa's School had to be replaced last year, and the parish was still shy some money to pay off the large debt. Father Joe agreed to be on the receiving end of many good natured jokes from reminiscing childhood friends, other priests, people from other parishes at which he had served, people from St. Theresa's who love him for all he did for their parish during the years he was there and his replacement, Father David. Each person who spoke was sure to begin with a funny, sometimes embarrassing, story that he or she was willing to share about Father Joe to bust him up, but every ending was the same. It was a "thank you" to their friend for all he had done for them, their families, their churches, their schools and the children. Every word was spoken with love for this man, my "boy."

At the conclusion of the roast, I determinedly made my way through the throngs of people in line to say "hello" to Father Joe Paquette. He hugged me, kissed my cheek and said, "Thank you for being a big part of my life." I was so thrilled that I repeated those words over and over in the car all the way home. I will never forget that my Joe said them to ME.

Father Joe and I are inside St. Theresa's Church
at my great-grandson Alex's christening.

1964 – I presented Liberace with the piano
cake at the Warwick Musical Tent.

My second meeting with Dennis Franz was in Newport.
Not to worry! His wife was right in back of him.

Butch Bussey took tap and ballet lessons from me then went on
to be asked to join the Royal Ballet. What talent he had.

Salty Brine, local TV and radio announcer, always "gave back," too. He would be at every fundraiser.

Another local TV and radio celebrity, Gene Degraide.

I visited the Dance Museum in Saratoga Springs, NY and
found the shoes of the great dancer George Raft.

Tommy Tune was starring in a Broadway show when I met
him backstage. In one picture, I stood on a chair.

In the other, I wanted people to see how tall he was.

On one of my Las Vegas trips to see the shows, I asked Englebert Humperdink and Macio, one of the "Stepbrothers," to pose for me.

Kathy and I went downtown Pawtucket to Meet Dustin Hoffman on the set of "American Buffalo."

My first meeting with Dennis Franz on the set.

Frankie Laine, singer.

Frankie Laine sang at Blinstraub's in Boston when I first
met him. We stayed friends over the years.

On one of my trips to London, I went to see "The
Phantom of the Opera" and met Hayley Mills.

Jimmy Durante made me laugh hysterically with his famous "HA-CHA-CHA." He was a star for sure.

In New York I was at a show and Alice Faye, a famous movie star, was with her poodle, Tili. I was never too shy to introduce myself.

HAPPY TIMES

I owe a lot of happiness to a lot of people for the unbelievable amount of time they put in to making me feel so special. One of those times was when my secretary, Kathy, decided I deserved an 80th birthday party. The reason was probably because not that many people can boast about being on this earth for eight decades and still be dancing strong. She called my daughter, and Susan made the phone calls to all who were invited. What a wonderful party I had at Twin Oaks Restaurant. But who knew I would have another iconic birthday party one decade later. SURPRISE!!!

And what a surprise it was. For my 90th birthday (while still dancing at the studio, by the way), Donna Carter and Fran Golombiewski, two of my former teachers who had been with me the longest, gave me a night to remember. There were over one hundred people invited to the Via Roma restaurant on Federal Hill, all clapping and singing "Happy Birthday," as I walked into the room. I was in total shock, having no clue that this was for me. But when I did, I loved every minute of it. After meeting and greeting everyone from family to friends to Mayor Grebien from Pawtucket, I sat at the main table which was decorated with signature top hats and miniature tap shoes. The meal was scrumptious and the entertainment stupendous! The Edwards Twins, male and female impersonators who have a show in Las Vegas, mesmerized everyone with their one and a half hour act as they impersonated such stars as Sonny and Cher, Neil Diamond, Bette Midler, Elton John, Barbra Streisand and others. When they are in Rhode Island, they perform at the Via Roma, the Odeum Theatre in East Greenwich, The Stadium Theatre in Woonsocket and other venues. It was a wonderful way to celebrate my 90th year – being entertained without having to write the play bill, plan the staging of the acts, or design the costumes. I just had to sit back and enjoy. And ENJOY I did!

It is almost five years later, and I can't stop thinking of MORE people in my life. When I look at my toes or fingernails, Gladdy is smiling at me in color. Always a cute smile on that face since the day I met her twenty-four years ago when her mother brought her in for lessons at the age of six. She stayed with me until she was twelve. What an entertainer she was. She did the "Black Face Dance" in recitals and shows when she was 7, 8 and 9, singing and dancing to "Mammie." Each time, she tore the house down. The audience always gave her a standing ovation.

Gladys "Gladdy" Michael's mother was from England and her father from India. Her mother sent her to live in India for a while with her father, but the hard part of her life was spent in 12 foster homes when she was just an infant. By the time she came to me, she was a very quiet little girl who found a love of the stage rise from within herself. Her parents were very strict with her rehearsing at home, but she didn't care. She loved the performing part.

Currently, Gladdy works, goes to school and manages to find time for me. She attended my friend Ace's funeral and met Sandy Strezak who, later, offered her a job. Sandy puts on children's competitions all over the state. She is the one who makes sure everything goes smoothly, books the rooms for the affairs and orders anything that is needed for the evening (props, etc.). She hired Gladdy to help her with these functions. Gladdy is, also, enrolled in courses at New England Technical Institute, studying for a degree in a medical field. And when I need a manicure and/ or a pedicure, Gladdy is at the door with her foot bucket and her choice of various colored polish which is the reason I said that I am reminded of her when I see the color on my nails.

Gladdy provides me with another source of help since I don't drive anymore. She knows how much I love my beach house, and she drives me there for a couple of days when no one is renting and she has vacation time. We both get to relax, as I stay on the porch with the windows wide open, breathing in the clean, salt air, while Gladdy jumps into the ocean, then walks the beach, her toes gripping the grainy sand.

And here she is performing her famous "Mammie" act.

MORE? HELP!

I will never forget Richard and all he has done for me. There would not be as many pictures in this book if Richard hadn't given me rides to Staples. On some Sundays, Richard picks me up to take me to Susan's house so I can see her and my great grandson, Alex, while Susan is busy cooking for all of us. I know I can count on Richard if I need an unscheduled ride to the doctor's office. These things that Richard does are proof of what a great person he is. He helps people (that includes me) in any way he can. Susan met Richard Osterman when they were both therapists working for The Providence Center. They have been friends for many years now, and if either of them needs a helping hand, the other is there to lend one.

Richard is a patient, kind and sensitive man. GOD BLESS HIM!

Richard's winning smile is obvious as he dines with Susan.

Another person who deserves a special thank you is George Leonard. Whatever would I have done without him? It was George I could rely on to put the music together for my shows right up until those last minute changes or add-ons to the already long list. He would, then, get all the music on cassette tapes and hand them to me with the biggest smile that screamed the word "YEA!" He had done it again! George played the piano for me at some of the recitals, too. His music was sacred to him, just as he was a Godsend to me.

WAIT! SO MANY MORE, SO FEW PAGES

There are more people I must mention in this book, people who have come and gone and have come back again into my life or my thoughts in some way. They, too, will always hold a special place in my heart for the roles they played in my life when they were on this earth. They still live in my thoughts on a regular basis.

The first person who passed on much too early was John DeGoes. The DeGoes family lived next door from the very day I bought the house on Shawmut Avenue. Mary, John's mother, was the nicest, kindest woman imaginable. When Susan began school at Mercymount, Mary would be waiting for her at the door when the bus dropped her off. She welcomed my daughter into her home, knowing the situation with Joe. Mary knew I had to return to work and make money, and she offered to watch Susan until I would get home from the studio. Her son, John, became a very big part of our lives, almost like a brother to Susan. After all, they ate dinner together every night and would share the stories of their days' activities. He was the sweetest, most well-mannered boy who would gladly do anything asked of him.

John's avocation was to become a teacher which later led to his being named the Superintendent of Schools in Central Falls. Due to the nature of his profession, John knew almost everyone in the city and was respected by all. After he married and moved out of his mother's house, I would look forward to seeing and talking with him when he visited. A thrill for Susan was when he was on the stage at her graduation from Rhode Island College and was the one to hand her diploma to her when she received her master's degree. Unfortunately, John's early demise in his early 70's was a great loss for the many people who knew him.

Another person I think of often is my old friend Shorty James. He, too, played the piano at many recitals. Shorty was an accomplished pianist who simply loved playing, whether it be for a show, in a club or just for fun. He liked to make people happy. Shorty "tickled the ivories" many nights at "The Music Room" on Hope Street in Providence while people danced and sang along with the music. One thing I'll always remember is I never saw

Shorty eat a real meal. He did love Twinkies. It seems that they were his main sustenance.

A woman who became a very good friend was Joan Rivet. She was a writer for The Pawtucket Times. Whenever she heard about a show I was putting on or anything she could say about things I had done for the city of Pawtucket, she would write a praiseworthy article about it in the paper. She would make sure to include the words "Theresa Landry and her dance school," knowing how much I loved showing off my kids. I have a very nice picture of her later on in her life when she was living in the housing for the elderly. I was devastated when I received a call one night at the studio informing me that Joan had been taken to Memorial Hospital and was asking for me. By the time I rushed there, I was just minutes late to say goodbye to a wonderful, talented woman and peer.

John and Jeanne DeGoes – John was a neighbor of love.

Shorty could think up a tune for anything. I wonder
what was going through his mind here.

The wonderful Joan Rivet is greeting my little 3 year old star,
Lynne Allen, at a show where Joan was a resident.

The following gallery of pictures is a compilation of all the topics I have covered throughout the book. They are not in any particular order on purpose. After having read the previous chapters and vignettes, I am almost certain that the pictures will jar your memory pertaining to the stories. However, if not, I know you will enjoy going back and finding the written word. I handpicked each picture and treasure every one of them.

GALLERY

My dad and I saw this horse and buggy as we were driving. It brought back so many memories. We asked someone to take our picture.

Every Sunday was dinner at my mother and
father's home. They loved Susan.

If there was wood around, my dad would find it.

Mom was living with me at this birthday moment.

My parents are entering the hall and having
dinner at their 50th anniversary party.

The Landry Sisters circa the '60s.

Irene is holding her novel at the Attic Owl Book Shop
in Moncton, N.B. September 27, 2001.

Bertha is dressed in the coat and hood I designed
for her for Susan's January wedding.

My granddaughter, Marisa, worked for me. I am so proud of her.

Susan is with her first born, Justin, a successful family man.

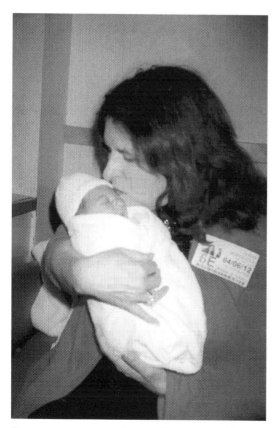

Susan loves every minute of newborn, Alexander,
my first great-grandson, my "little fella."

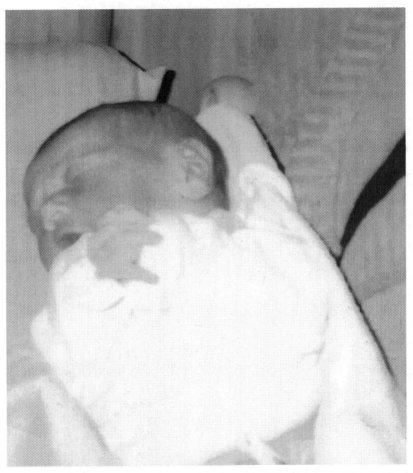

When Alexander was born, he would cross his little hands as if he were praying. I thought maybe he would be a priest! He's 5 now and I think NOT.

Alex wanted a firetruck cake for this birthday. Looks like Marisa had to blow the candle out.

A happy, loving couple, Marisa and Tom are
at Justin and Michelle's wedding.

Susan is with my second great-grandson,
Michael. Another "little fella" to love.

A joyous day for me. Michele, Justin, and I at Michael's christening.

In this great-grandson Michael's collage, his happy smile shines
except for the first picture in his snowsuit! Michael is now 4
years old and plays t-ball. He still has that adorable smile.

This is the last time all three sisters were together for a picture.
It's my favorite because of Justin and Marisa being in it.

Susan and I are at a gala affair.

A real mom and dad family photo. From left to right, in back
is Irene with her son Hugh in front, mom with Bertha's son
Tom in front, me with Susan in front, Dad with Bertha's son
Bob in front and Bertha with her son Dan in front.

Ronnie enjoyed going to fancy dress up places.

I love Paris! Being so close to the Eiffel Tower
was a dream come true in 1979.

Russia was absolutely divine! This is Moscow.

Just a few years ago, Susan and I went on a car trip
to Maine, absolutely beautiful scenery.

The Spanish castanet rolling dancers show off my love of the color red and how I enjoy designing skirts with layers of ruffles.

I just knew that Fran Gorman would look stunning in this fitted floral design.

Three of my best teachers, Gail, Denise, and Fran, had the
perfect bodies for these feather and glitter costumes.

I love feathers. They're so light on your head. This
particular headpiece is one of my favorites.

It's true, a mirror is the eye of the soul. My designed
hats always showed me having fun.

Susan and I in the front, leading the tap dancing girls wearing their white gloves, with a third design of feathered costumes in the back.

The float we made for parades in Central Falls and Pawtucket
has the girls (Marisa far left) in their country costumes. You
can see the Jenckes Park clock in the background.

Somehow, I managed to get one of the men to be spray painted in gold, representing my Oscar winning students.

Susan Nessie and Lynne Kwarcinski in their leopard print costumes.

In 1985, Lynne Kwarcinski wore the leopard costume and tall, feathered headpiece in the show. She doesn't seem like she dislikes it in our picture.

I made it up to Lynne in later years by presenting her with flowers.

The 1776 girls coming down the stairs at the Armory were so impressive.

The 1776 girls as they walked down the aisle. At
table on right is then Mayor Dennis Lynch.

I had to improvise the hats which I bent and folded from straw ones.

Watching Eddie Boudessa was a treat. He was so limber. During this act, he was flanked by me on his left and Susan on his right.

Susan got to wear the famous headpiece as she was escorted on stage.

A beautiful bevy of girls from left to right: Robin Lynn Vassar, Cathy Ormond, Susan De Vonis, Fran Golombiewski, Stephanie Caccieri, Lynne Kwarcinski, and Denise Dauphinais.

Susan and I went to the George M. Cohan tribute to see
Kevin get the award. I will always be there for him.

Kevin, Donna, and I flew to Florida to relax with my sister, Bertha.
We wined, dined, and enjoyed each other's company.

A great couple and great friends.

Before the trip to Washington, I made Kevin a cake for dessert after dinner in my dining room. No one could ever resist that smile.

Kevin never said "no" to me, not even when I asked him to be part of the Pawsox show. He's always right there for me.

I couldn't resist showing off a little leg myself in Washington.

My girls danced at a dinner in honor of Governor
and Mrs. Phillip Nael in 1975

My Senior Line danced at the State House for then Governor John
Chafee. After, he agreed to a picture on the State House steps.

My mother was so happy to meet Buddy Cianci. It was the beginning of a good friendship between myself and the Mayor of Providence.

Buddy matched the 1776 costumes that the girls wore
at Providence City Hall. He liked the kiss, too.

Mayor Cianci was fun to be around. We had our picture
taken at a fundraiser in front of the United States flag.

Bob was running for office when Anthony and I went
to a dinner for him. His wife was so sweet.

Bob had another fundraiser/dinner at the Providence Marriott Hotel. Susan and Linda joined us and I brought a cake with Bob's likeness imprinted on it.

Betty Leonard ran for governor of Rhode Island. Anthony and I were friends with her and her husband, Ted, who owned the Auto Show Volvo dealership. Here we are in his long, white Cadillac. Anthony is in the driver's deat, Betty in passenger seat, and Susan, Me, and Ted are in the back.

Here's a closeup of Betty Leonard during her campaign
days with Anthony, myself, and Susan.

Ted, Vickie, and Patrick Kennedy were all very gracious people.

Before she owned her own restaurant, my sister, Bertha, waitressed at a restaurant in New York frequented by Bobby Kennedy. She, too, loved to be photographed with politicians.

Presidential hopeful, at the time, Bill Clinton was a charmer.

Riding in the buggy with the horses trotting down the street by
Central Park in New York with Kathy and Kim has always been
a special treat either before or after seeing "The Rockettes," my
favorite Christmastime show. I plan on seeing yet another one.

Kim took this picture of me and Kathy at Trump Towers.
Look at the beauty of the plants (and the two women!)

Donna Carter and Fran Golombiewski, teachers and former students
who opened their own studios, help celebrate my 80th birthday.

I thanked Jeanne Corvese so many times for getting all those nomination names for me to be in the Pawtucket Hall of Fame.

The jazz music was great every night when
Anthony and I went to New Orleans.

While taking a boat ride, I had to take this picture of Anthony. He looked like a sexy model with the wind blowing through his hair.

Christmas with Anthony was always a day full of fun, joy, presents, and love.

Anthony had many interests, politics being one of
them. That's another reason I loved him.

Baby, it was cold outside this restaurant where we waited
to get in to attend a rally for Betty Leonard.

While in Italy, we met and joked with the real "Alfredo" at his restaurant.

I would enjoy a nice, relaxing bath at the end of each day.

After the long, luxurious bath comes the rest
and rejuvenation for the next day.

Anthony and I had taken a ride to Rockport to enjoy my
favorite food, lobster, at Captain Peg Legs.

This picture marks our last Christmas together, so sad, in my living room.

A student and fantastic teacher and still a great
friend, Gloria Dorais with her husband, Al.

It's important to have mirrors on all the walls in a dance studio. Whoever took this pic of me in my director's chair shows this perfectly.

I always loved to entertain in my finished basement. There are so many things I bought over the years and in various countries. From floor to ceiling, you can see them here: furniture, vases, rugs, statues.

Giving Susan and Linda a party at The Music Room
when they received their Masters degrees in counseling
was a treat for me, as was this cake for all.

I celebrated my 90th birthday with my family at Trattoria Restaurant.
The women in my life are Susan, Marisa, Michelle, and the
little fellas are Michael being hugged by Alexander.

My Susan and Linda made me happy to be able to celebrate such a day.

The real 90th birthday surprise occurred when I walked into the Via Roma with Donna and Fran. This surprise will never be matched.

Examples of Play Bills and Tickets

THERESA LANDRY
✸ School of Dancing ✸
"Hall of Fame"

Presents-

EXTRAVAGANZA 2000

Sunday, November 5   2:00 pm
North Providence High School
North Providence, Rhode Island

A Special Thanks To My Right Hand Girl
Without Her It Wouldn't Be Possible
"The Boss" Kathy Zabek
Love Theresa

To Kevin Doyle "Educated Feet"
Never Stop Dancing - You're The Greatest

To Kim Audette... A Most Dedicated Teacher And Loyal
Friend!

To My Grandaughter Marisa... We Miss You
Luck and Love, Grandma

A Special Thanks To Ashley Marra - Acro Teacher

Erica Chan - Assistant Teacher
MIT Here I Come...Congratulations!

THERESA LANDRY
Producer - Teacher - Choreographer

Born   **Theresa**

To   **Age**

Dance   **3**

Theresa Landry School of Dancing
100 Dexter Street, Pawtucket, Rhode Island
Excepting New Students - Call
401-726-9083

Sunday, June 7   at 7:30 p. m.

FOOT-STEPS OF 1953

Presented by

Theresa Landry's School of Dancing

East Senior High School Auditorium
Exchange Street, Pawtucket, R. I.
"*Sponsored by the Four Leaf Clover Club*"

Tickets $1.20 tax included

THERESA LANDRY

presents

EXTRAVAGANZA "78"

& Her Talented Young Artists

June 18, 1978   at 2:00 p.m.

at Veteran's Memorial
Providence. R. I.

Adults — $3.50
Children Under 5 Free

Free Parking
across from State House

NOW IT'S MY TURN

I decided that writing this epilogue would be the only way in which I (the Ghost Writer) would ever get my own two cents worth of words into Theresa's book. I hope it has been obvious how much I enjoyed listening to the stories that Theresa told me as I sat with her for hours sometimes in her dining room, sometimes in her kitchen and sometimes in her living room. Each time I would get to her house with anticipation, for I never knew what was going to come out of her mouth next. Would I hear tales of her parents, her friends, her family? Often, we would look at the black book she had on the dining room table which contains years of her hand written notes about all these subjects and more. Now it is my turn to tell my stories about...

THERESA, KNOWN THROUGHOUT THE LIFE OF THE GHOST WRITER.

Susan and I became best friends on the first day of the first grade at Mercymount Country Day School. It was destiny! Both our last names began with the letter "S," with me sitting in front of her. I turned around, even though Sister Mary Alquin had told us to "Face front," and saw the same look of fear in this little girl's eyes as I knew was in mine.

As the school year progressed, our friendship grew. One wintry day in February the snow began to fall heavily after the bus had deposited us at the school. By the time lunch was over, we were told that the busses would be taking us home early due to the snow piling higher by the hour. Immediately, a great idea entered my mind. I asked Susan if she would like to get off the bus at my stop and come to my house to play paper dolls. Of course she said yes. What five year old wouldn't?

By 5o'clock that afternoon, Theresa was a wreck. She had heard on the radio that schools were closing, but Susan had never made it home. After many calls to the convent from a sobbing Theresa and many calls to the bus company and, eventually, to the police by the nuns, Sister Alquin thought to call Susan's friend Linda's house. I answered, surprised to hear my teacher's voice, and said, "Yes, Sister, Susan is here. Want to talk to her?" After a quick exchange of words, Theresa was at my house in a heartbeat, kissing and hugging her "little Susie." I witnessed a mother's love for her daughter that can never be compared.

Theresa's giving nature was actually lucky for me, too. When Susan turned sixteen and got her driver's license, a brand new baby blue Chevy Impala convertible with a white top and white interior was purchased by "Guess Who?" Why was this lucky for me? Susan broke her right ankle that summer, and I had to drive her, in the gorgeous car, to her doctors' appointments. I NEVER complained, especially when we would take side trips to Newport Creamery for ice cream or Del's Lemonade or ride by the local Burger Chef to see if any cute boys were around. No, I never complained about Theresa's generosity and faith in me.

However, Theresa made sure that Susan understood the concept of working to get the things you want in life. By making a quick call to one of her student's mothers, Ethel Boudessa, Theresa secured summer jobs for both Susan and I at Hassenfeld's, now known as Hasbro, a mill on Newport Avenue in Pawtucket. We worked mothers' hours, 9 to 3, and our job was to put together toy hairdryers as they came flying at us on the conveyor belt. Some days the heat in this brick monstrosity was unbearable with no air conditioning, just little fans at the top of a very high ceiling. We had fifteen minutes for lunch and one five minute ladies' room run. Through Theresa, we certainly learned the meaning of never thinking you could get something for nothing. The concepts of hard work and saving money were instilled in both of us. Notably, these were concepts that Theresa had been taught during her own life.

There have been many "Theresa" stories in my life over the years, but the best is the most recent. When I began ghost writing this book and going to Theresa's house on a regular basis, I learned the true value of listening. Just as I loved hearing my father's stories about his family and their farms in Canada, his World War II adventures in the army and the many people in his life, since he was self-employed, also, I relearned that same attitude toward Theresa as I would leave the house feeling her emotions by hearing them through her words. These are the same words of wisdom that people from my father's and Theresa's generation passed down to their children. After having lived through the Depression, they learned the meaning of sacrifice and hard work. Theresa knew when it was time to stop and smell the roses when necessary, as well. Her futuristic mentality brought her years of joy with her family, her daughter, her grandchildren, her students, her summer house and, now, her great grandchildren. Nothing was easy, but she knew how to make it look that way.

As I sit here writing, my mind cannot help but wander to where Theresa is today. At the beginning of this summer, as she descended the stairs in her house, she miscalculated the last step, fell and broke her hip. While in the ER and after some lovely pain killers, she was told that the doctor would be in to assess the damage shortly. Her immediate response to Susan and myself was, "I hope he's an older gentleman so I can flirt." Her sense of humor is amazing, even when she is thrown a bad curve. This is the Theresa I have known and always admired...the positive woman, the one who never gives up.

After recuperating at St. Antoine's Home in North Smithfield, receiving daily physical therapy and walking with the aid of a walker, Theresa is living with Susan and loving all the attention and friends dropping by. Since day one of the writing of this book of her life, Theresa has told me how she wants the last words to read:

"WHAT'S NEXT, GOD?"

ACKNOWLEDGEMENT

I would like to give a special "shout out" to Stacy Coletti for all the time and effort she put into working on inserting all the pictures and captions in their proper order throughout the book. Stacy, to whom I am deeply grateful, is a gifted, talented computer artist who takes great pride in her work.

Printed in the United States
By Bookmasters